SWEET
PARIS

SWEET PARIS

SEASONAL RECIPES FROM

AN AMERICAN BAKER IN FRANCE

FRANK ADRIAN BARRON

PHOTOGRAPHS BY JOANN PAI

An Imprint of HarperCollins Publishers

SWEET PARIS

HarperCollins books may be purchased for educational,
business, or sales promotional use. For information,
please email the Special Markets Department at
SPsales@harpercollins.com.

First published in 2022 by
Harper Design
An Imprint of HarperCollins*Publishers*
195 Broadway
New York, NY 10007
Tel: (212) 207-7000
Fax: (855) 746-6023
harperdesign@harpercollins.com
hc.com

Distributed throughout the world by
HarperCollins*Publishers*
195 Broadway
New York, NY 10007

ISBN 978-0-06-304023-6
Library of Congress Control Number: 2021041048

Book design by Amanda Jane Jones
Photographs by Joann Pai
Styling Assistant Kate Devine
Photographs on pages 23, 57, 81 by Frank Adrian Barron
Photograph on page 121 by Kevin Aldrich
Illustrations by Rosie Kiser Jones

Printed in Malaysia

First Printing, 2022

For James

contents

introduction

MY STORY STARTS WITH STRAWBERRIES. Or, more specifically, a lack thereof.

We moved to Paris in January 2012—my now-husband, James, our bewildered Boston Terrier, Parker, and myself—departing a mild California and touching down on a blustery cold France, covered in snow.

It was to be a temporary move. James had received an interesting job offer. And since I legally wouldn't be able to work, I decided to take the time to study the language. It was all a fabulous opportunity we simply couldn't pass up. It was the City of Light, after all: magical even when iced over, and full of wintertime charm. We kicked the slush off our shoes as we entered our warm apartment for the first time and started our next chapter as Parisians.

As with any move, we spent the initial few weeks getting into the swing of what our normal life would be. That meant figuring out James's commute on the metro, finding parks for Parker, and doing the basics, like unpacking, setting up utilities, and most important, scoping out local grocery stores.

Around the corner from us, I spotted a Monoprix, the French equivalent of the American Target chain, and grabbed my warmest coat and a shopping list to go scan the aisles for the items we'd regularly have in our kitchen. Despite still being new to French, I could find some items without any aid. Eggs. Herbal tea. Milk. Yogurt. But when it came to the fruit topping I wanted for that yogurt, I was stumped.

Strawberries were nowhere to be found.

In broken Franglais, I asked a clerk where to find them. She looked at me, confused. I assumed she didn't understand me, so I repeated my question, pronouncing it as precisely as I could. She groaned. "C'est pas possible, monsieur!" she responded, incredulous. "Ce n'est pas la saison!"

I pieced together what she'd said, word by word. Strawberries were not possible. It was "not the season."

Strawberries . . . impossible? She was speaking to a man from California, where, all year round, you could find almost any fruit for every bowl of yogurt or any type of smoothie you desired. Moreover, she was speaking to an American, whose country proudly includes strawberry next to vanilla and chocolate as one of its most treasured ice cream flavors. Had she ever heard of the classic triple threat that is a cone full of Neapolitan?

To me, strawberries were standard. And I thought we'd just moved to the country claiming to be the capital of all things "food." I felt shocked—and soon thereafter, culture shocked: The French, I'd quickly find out, preferred to eat by the season, buying fruits and vegetables right when they're harvested, when their flavor is at its natural peak. Though I was aware of this practice in theory, it wasn't how we ate where I was from, a land with everything available at any time.

It had been my faux pas (how French of me), and the moment I realized my thinking needed to shift to seasonality. Strawberries, I'd learn, wouldn't appear until the end of spring or start of summer. The fresh asparagus on my list? Also not available until springtime. Oranges and clementines? Here now, but it's the end of the season, so enjoy them while you can. And the figs James had requested? Gone, but back come fall.

I'd have to get used to it. If my yogurt required strawberries, it would also require patience. It was the first lesson my new country taught me.

France is a country that likes to adhere to rules. That's the second thing I learned from living here. And these rules are never more apparent than in the French approach to food, from how you slice cheese to how you present bread (hint: never upside down, as it's considered bad luck, and always directly on the table, not on a plate).

Rules also extend to snacking, or goûter (pronounced "goo-tay"). Unlike Americans, who might be okay with snacking whenever they want, the French have a strictly defined snack time called *l'heure du goûter*. Like strawberries arriving in May and not January, there is an appropriate window in which to enjoy a snack: between 4 and 5 pm, the afterschool hour, because goûter (also called *le quatre heures*) is traditionally meant for children being picked up from school, returning home. It's a sight I often see: When I take the newest member of our family, Fitz, for his afternoon walk, little kids run by with sticky fingers thanks to something chocolatey like a pain au chocolat brought to them by an indulgent grown-up. I've been told it's a way for kids to sustain themselves until supper, as the French tend to eat dinner later than Americans do. To be sure, the goûter hour isn't only enjoyed by kids. Adults of all ages find themselves hankering for something sweet around that late afternoon hour, a holdover from childhood.

Unbeknownst to me, I'd been practicing the art of goûter, against the rules, early on in my time in Paris. When we first moved to the city, I took French language classes at La Sorbonne, and both before and after class, I'd pick up a new-to-me pastry. That means I wasn't paying particular attention to the hour at which I was indulging. Walking from my school, located near the Luxembourg Gardens, and back over to our apartment in the Marais, I got to know all the French grands classiques—from the decadent Paris-Brest, a wheel of choux pastry filled with praliné-flavored buttercream and created in honor of a famous bicycle race from Paris to Brest, to the divine St. Honoré, a pastry topped with cream puffs that have been dipped in caramelized sugar and named for the patron saint of pastry chefs, to the flaky chausson aux pommes, buttery puff pastry baked until golden and filled with apples. Whether the rules came naturally to me or not, I've since become a loyal adherent to the goûter philosophy. Not a day goes by, whether at home in Paris or on holiday elsewhere, that I forego the sacred ritual. In essence, it's a moment to pause, a moment to focus on pure pleasure.

For me, my version of l'heure du goûter also extended to coffee. And I don't mean just any cuppa: I mean having a high-quality, locally roasted cup in a specialty shop. It wasn't something easy to find at the time, as coffee-shop culture was a scene that was only kicking off in Paris when we arrived. It was an odd experience to not have an excellent flat white or a beautifully poured cappuccino anywhere nearby, especially as we relocated from San Francisco, a city that takes coffee very seriously.

When I wasn't in class, I'd often spend afternoons on my own in one of the two coffee spots available: Coutume, on the other side of the Seine in the 7th arrondissement, and Kooka Boora (now KB CaféShop), up by Sacré-Cœur. It took me two metro trains—and a half hour—to enjoy either. But I had no qualms about it because it was the kind of caffeination I craved. And as these shops, and ones that soon followed, were either expat-owned or inspired by Third Wave cafés from the likes of Australia, the UK, and the US, I found in them a bubble of comfort. These were places filled not only with the best brews but also with other expats. Moreover, these shops wanted to cater to their clientele, so instead of offering ubiquitous French pastries to accompany the coffee, they put out something unique: American-style baked goods like banana bread and cookies.

It was a good thing. Because after I'd gorged myself on all the French delicacies available, I was ready for tastes that reminded me of home. And as we soon learned that we'd be staying in Paris indefinitely, I was also ready to find ways to feel a little less alone.

As any expat will tell you, the first year away is the hardest. When we moved to Paris, I didn't know anyone. After a year, I still hadn't made a community of friends. Fortunately, however, excellent coffee came in to save the day. My timing was lucky: More and more expat-led coffee shops began opening, and with our dog Parker as my sidekick, I'd wander over to check them out. And the thing is, if you put excellent coffee in front of me and get me gabbing, I guarantee we'll be friends before that cup is empty.

While I worked on the friendships I'd been missing, I also happened to be working on replicating the tastes of home I missed, too. The ubiquitous loaves of banana bread and chocolate chip cookies on the counters of these coffee shops, some of which were run by foreigners accustomed to American-style baked goods, did help, but there was one particular thing I wanted.

Coffee's most reliable sidekick. Cake, American-style. Because, while the French excel at fine pâtisserie and breakfast pastries like croissants and brioche, they were not reared with buttercream-filled layer cakes, cupcakes, and rainbow sprinkles. Locally, however, American and English specialty bake shops were emerging and, by extension, the Parisian palate was expanding. Heart emojis appeared on Parisian eyes when they discovered iced carrot cakes (the earliest version was certainly the one served at Rose Bakery, the pioneer of the English-style canteen), cheesecakes, and scones served with cream and jam.

Despite the handy new bolt-holes churning out cheesecake and blueberry muffins, I still rarely saw the cakes I craved most: yellow layer cake covered in chocolate buttercream, or squares of cinnamon-laced coffee cake topped with a crunchy streusel topping. So slowly, I began trying my hand at baking. Though I hadn't baked much back in California, my mom had taught me a few things when I was growing up in San Diego. Somewhere in the back of my mind, I knew how to properly grease and line a cake pan. I could also recall how to shake a pan out with flour. But I was going to need to engage in a lot of practicing to be able to make all of the confections I was missing most.

The basics I learned from my mom gave me the confidence to attempt simple things, like loaf cakes, brownies, cupcakes, and thanks to some Nordic Ware in my cookware arsenal from the States, beaucoup Bundt cakes. I liked Bundts because they were easy and straightforward but can look complicated due to the beautiful mold. (And for added flair, you can add a glaze that drips down the side.) I especially remember making a cinnamon–brown sugar Bundt (page 111), a cake my mom often baked for us. It delivered everything I wanted it to. It was nostalgic. It made me feel a little less homesick. And it was fun.

From then on, I was hooked.

Best of all? I now had friends with whom to share my newfound skills. Excited to play host again, I began inviting them over to the apartment for a goûter in what I called "cake parties." It gave me a chance to test out new recipes—often using fresh, seasonal ingredients—and it helped me solidify the new relationships I'd formed.

I even earned myself a title: "Cake Boy," a nickname a few friends once jokingly called me at a party here in France. It's from a scene in the movie *Clueless*, the seminal classic from 1996, where Christian, the character Alicia Silverstone's Cher is in love with, turns out to be gay.

"Your man Christian is a cake boy!" Cher's friend tells her. "He's a disco-dancing, Oscar Wilde–reading, Streisand-ticket-holding friend of Dorothy, know what I'm saying?"

When that film came out, I was a teenager. I recall thinking, "'Cake boy?' Never heard of it." I'm sure the term was originally meant disparagingly; but now, I liked the idea of taking it back. I also loved how the once derogatory term was meant to evoke everything a cake can be: over-the-top, fancy, sweet, decadent, and dramatic.

"I adore cake. And I'm a cake boy," I thought. "Plus I appreciate a double entendre . . . so, I'll own it."

From that point on, cakes I made at home got photographed and posted on Instagram at @cakeboyparis.

For a period of about six months, it was all about more, more, more. More cakes baked. More parties to celebrate those cakes. And more friends made, including several of the expat owners of the coffee-based cafés I now regularly frequented.

One Australian I'd befriended was Chris Nielson, who owned Fondation Café, a tiny specialty coffee shop in the Marais offering perfectly poured café cremes. In late summer 2014, I stopped by for a goûter, as I often did. It was August, the time in Paris when everything shuts down and almost everyone leaves for vacation—and Fondation was one of the few brave shops that remained open to serve people like us who'd stayed in town. Funny enough, Chris was on vacation, too, but had hired a couple friends to stay behind to run the café. When I got to the counter and said bonjour, there were no baked goods. "Our bakers are on holiday like everyone else," the barista explained to me. "We won't have anything for a couple weeks."

Sacrilège! The word swirled through my head. Whatever would I eat with my coffee?

"Not even a cookie?" I asked. He must have sensed my panic, because the barista immediately asked if I knew someone they could pay to bake something, perhaps a banana bread or a cake?

I wasn't sure if he was serious. I asked him to repeat it. And when he did, Cake Boy responded.

"Yes, I *do* know someone," I said—and I was on my way to creating my first cake for a Paris coffee shop.

It was the third lesson Paris taught me: Yes. Just say yes.

The barista gave me carte blanche to create whatever I wanted. I made a very dainty raspberry lemon tea cake with a pink glaze, topped with seasonal summertime raspberries. I brought the cake over to the café that weekend; I even had James take a photo of me walking it there.

"One slice, please," I said after delivering it. I ate it in front, at a table on the sidewalk, sipping a fresh brew, happy as a clam. I was glad I'd said yes. The final product might have had an uneven glaze and lost a raspberry or two on the walk over, but it felt satisfying to have done it. And if nothing else, I got to have cake with my coffee.

So did I ultimately bake that first cake for selfish reasons? Probably. I figured it was a one-off thing. I had no aspirations to bake cakes in any professional capacity. But because we're now in the age of social media, a few people stopped by and took photos of the cake. And I began to get Instagram notices that @cakeboyparis had been tagged.

I gradually attempted more complicated layer cakes. I wanted to re-create the kinds of cakes I grew up with . . . those that can hold a hefty layer of buttercream and rainbow sprinkles and wish you a happy birthday at the same time. My initial iterations were wonky and disheveled, of course. I didn't know how to do all the minor things that make a cake look more professional— correctly stacking the layers, adding a crumb coat, or even properly cutting a slice.

As I started to invest in a few baking books and practice my skills using online videos, I received some inquiries from people who saw the cake I made for Fondation Café on Instagram. "Do you make cakes for coffee shops?" they'd ask. "Could you make one for us?"

That's when my cakes started showing up in select coffee spots around Paris.

One of my first cake pop-ups was for Boot Café, a former cobbler's shop turned specialty coffee shop, right around the corner from our apartment. The owner, an American, messaged me to do a unique treat for the weekend. I brought them my mom's cinnamon–brown sugar Bundt (topped with an elegant glaze and a spray of sunny yellow roses), then posted about it on social media. The majority of people who stopped by were my friends, of course, and the cake was gone in a few hours. I couldn't stop grinning, though. Gathering those friends around my mother's cake, enjoying it in the moment together, somehow felt meaningful to me.

Soon, thanks to Instagram and to those friends who like to chitchat with café owners over their coffee, other spots asked me to do pop-ups, too. I created cakes for places like Café Oberkampf, Loustic Café, and Honor Café, which had the, *ahem*, honor of displaying my first attempt at a layer cake. It was a simple blueberry swirl cake with a classic vanilla buttercream, decorated with flowers and sugared blueberries, a technique I'd only recently taught myself. Layer cakes like these, covered in buttercream, are rare occurrences in France, where birthdays are often celebrated with either a variety of fresh fruit tarts or a very simple pound cake.

And as these tales tend to go, those cakes in cafés led to private clients. They'd often be expats who'd tried my American-style layer cakes or Bundt cakes and asked a barista who made them. "Could you make me a birthday cake?" read their messages to me, time and again. Once, a couple even asked me to make their wedding cake.

Truth be told, I would doubt my capabilities when these inquiries came through. I'd feel like I couldn't do it. I'd scold myself for not taking it seriously enough or for not being a trained pastry chef. But I'd already seen where *oui* could take me, so I pushed myself to accept every new challenge.

Layer by layer, cake by cake, I then realized that saying yes had given me a gift: a creative outlet. I was filling my time having fun while learning new techniques and new types of cakes. On top of that, with social media, it became an opportunity to improve my love of photography, a skill I already enjoyed exploring as a traveler.

But remember where my story started, with a lack of strawberries? That's the lesson that helped me take my artistic endeavor to the next level. That is how my baking started to soar.

For someone like me, coming from California, the initial thought I had about adjusting to seasonal eating was that I was now limited. I wouldn't be able to create whatever I'd want, whenever I wanted. But what I didn't expect was the discovery, excitement, and creativity it would offer me instead.

Certainly, there's joy in trying something new—a feeling you're no stranger to when you move to a foreign country. Not only did I learn when certain fruits and vegetables (and flowers!) would be in season and at their very best, I also added new tastes to my palate.

In fall, I now know to look for mirabelles, tiny golden-yellow plums that only appear for a short window of time. At markets in the winter, I seek chestnuts. And strawberries are a late spring/summertime arrival, but they're also not just "strawberries" like we have back home. There are varieties—and at the market, you must know what you want. Do you need sweet? Tart? Or do you prefer the tiny forest type? You'll hear names thrown about like gariguette, fraise des bois, fraise ronde, and la mara des bois. And, true to seasonal eating, these varieties arrive at different times in the season itself, so you have to stay in the know. Because if you're shopping and ask for fraise des bois a week too soon, be warned: That vendor might snap back with a roll of the eyes and a "Non, monsieur! Une semaine!"

I have also learned the joy of anticipation. When you've waited for that fresh clementine or artichoke or peony to finally appear in a market stall, you appreciate it that much more. When everyone knows it's the right moment to spotlight a particular item again, there's a special buzz

going around. "Great, we're moving into stone fruit season now!" is the sort of thing I catch myself thinking. "Soon there'll be peaches everywhere, plus all those varieties of nectarines and plums!"

That's when I get excited about coming up with ideas on how to use those items in my baking.

With every fruit that comes into season, it's a new chance for me to get imaginative. I brainstorm on walks with Fitz to grab a goûter or stay up late researching online. When the cherries are abundant at the market, I now wonder about making cherry tea cakes—or maybe cherry ice cream? When white peaches arrive, what could I do? Ah! Strawberries are here. Am I going to make a layer cake, muffins, or something breakfasty? (To be honest, probably all three.) I try to get the most out of a season while it's there—to celebrate it. And in turn, my cake making becomes more thoughtful.

Also, it becomes more delicious. When you use ingredients at the very height of their flavor, it elevates your baking, especially when you create something that lets that ingredient shine. For instance, there's a fallen fig cake recipe in my Autumn chapter (see page 129). It uses a simple cake base that's not too sweet, because the intention is that it shouldn't compete with the figs—it should allow the fruit flavor to be the star. You halve the fresh figs and place them face up in the batter as if they had just freshly fallen from a fig tree. As they bake, the figs caramelize deliciously in their natural juices. The cake spotlights the fig at its finest. I find it's a beautiful way to use up all of the bounty that's out in the markets come fall.

As my baking evolved, I evolved away from pop-ups at coffee shops and from private clients, reducing my customer list to only the occasional birthday cake. I wanted to discover a new challenge in the realm of cake making. And, as social media has often played a helpful role in this creative project of mine, it again lent a hand, this time in the form of inquiries about leading cake-decorating workshops.

I had never considered it. I felt like I was still in a learning phase (and imposter syndrome was still a struggle). However, the idea of welcoming people into my home for an afternoon of seasonal cake decorating, and more importantly, cake eating, seemed like fun! Moreover, I felt I had the perfect space to offer it. A few friends had used our apartment to hold successful food photography workshops (including Joann Pai, this book's wonderful photographer) so I had seen it in action.

My idea was that I would prepare layer cakes in advance, and then with a small group of people, we'd tie on aprons and make a frosting. Afterward, we'd stack those cakes, frost them, and I'd set out an array of flowers, berries, or fruits for the class to decorate the cakes, explaining how the items were in season and when I first spotted them at the market. Together, we'd swap suggestions and get creative. We'd also gab and gossip, with the occasional giggle if someone made a delightful mess, and a big cheer when someone felt they'd crafted their personal masterpiece.

After a few workshops, I couldn't help but smile. It all dawned on me. Teaching people about cakes had somehow naturally brought together all the ingredients of my journey in Paris: learning from the creativity of cake making; the joy of baking—and decorating—by season; the nostalgia of American baking, infused with the elegant sophistication I discovered in all those countless Parisian pastry shops; the beauty of an afternoon in Paris; and the gathering of new friends around something sweet. At the end of every workshop, I made sure we'd slice up the cake I had decorated and enjoy it together with a cup of tea or a sparkling glass of champagne.

Because now that I'm in France, I know to follow the rules. And my number one is that every day, you should always say yes to a seasonally sweet moment with a good goûter.

I hope this book—my love letter to time spent baking throughout the year in Paris—inspires you to do the same.

A NOTE ON CREATING A COOKBOOK IN THE TIME OF COVID

The theme of my book is baking by the season and gathering with friends to enjoy the sweet results. But I created it when time outside and at markets was limited, as was getting together with other people. Paris went into lockdown in March 2020, just as I'd started writing.

In a country where there are already lots of "rules," there were even more rules to life here, as there were in cities across the globe. The logistics of recipe creation became complicated. Though I never saw France's butter shortage, flour and different types of sugar were harder for me to find. We weren't allowed to travel more than one kilometer from our home, so I was unable to go across town for specialty ingredients. We could order items online, but it took longer for delivery. Most difficult of all, as the seasons shifted outside our windows, the rules continued to shift, sometimes preventing me from getting together with Joann, my good friend and the photographer of this book.

It was a challenge on the creative front, to say the least.

As everyone experienced in 2020, the emotional aspect was even more challenging. Other than the more existential elements—we all know how that felt—little thoughts would creep in. Would I still have a book to create? Should I even do it? Is this important? How could I get motivated to write about something as cheery as baking cakes when the world felt like it was falling apart?

Interestingly, I found comfort in baking. My mother's ever-present cinnamon–brown sugar Bundt cake was a regular feature on our afternoon table, often paired with a homemade cappuccino that took me nearly as long to make as the cake.

The world, it seems, had also found the same consolation. It was beautiful to watch home bakers emerging on social media as we all spent time living slower. Baking, as we've all learned, is an art form. It takes patience and preparation. You must check and recheck that you've correctly measured ingredients or timed the oven just right. And unlike cooking, baking can bring about a host of disappointments (I've faced them all!). But the elbow grease you put into it, I find, is worth it. Especially if it's taught you a lesson, allowed you to create something gorgeous, granted you the confidence to say yes to a new recipe, or simply given you a taste you remembered from growing up, at the moment you needed it most.

And while we're all still watching how the world will evolve as we move forward, my wish is that this book will bring you some insight—and inspiration—as we celebrate new seasons of gathering together around a table again.

A NOTE ON BUTTERCREAM

Buttercream making was an important teacher as I learned to adapt to baking as an American in France.

When I was regularly making cakes for coffee shops, I was in a steep learning curve, so I naturally asked for feedback from café owners. This was especially true at the newly opened Café Oberkampf, where friend and owner Guy Griffin wasn't yet offering pastry. There was a three-month period where he asked me to bring cakes almost every weekend.

"Make whatever you want," he'd say. "Whatever's in season would be spot-on."

I admittedly had some major cake fails, including times when I showed up with nothing in hand. But Guy stayed patient and made sure I understood what was working—and what wasn't.

And the thing that really didn't work? American buttercream.

"Some of the European customers don't understand the buttercream, as it's really sweet," he explained. "They're leaving it on the plate and not finishing it all."

Leaving it behind? Buttercream, the most beloved part of a cake experience? My American friends and I felt cake was simply a vehicle to deliver the frosting. Just give us a bowl of the sweet stuff and we'd be happy.

It was another cultural moment. The American classic was much too much.

I started researching other frostings that might satisfy their tastes. I knew about whipped cream frosting, but I also knew it didn't go with everything. That's when two European beauties crossed my path: Swiss meringue buttercream and Italian meringue buttercream. They are both luscious, rich, and very buttery—yet vastly less sweet than their American counterpart.

As I started to practice creating them, I noticed they required a bit more effort than the American version. Swiss meringue buttercream involves cooking eggs and sugar over a double boiler before adding in the butter, where Italian meringue requires you to boil a sugar syrup, whip egg whites into a meringue, and slowly add bits of butter. It's a longer, more complicated process, but the end result is a mildly sweet buttercream that's perfect for stacking and filling layer cakes.

I quickly incorporated these new frostings into my cakes. And yes, they were a much bigger hit with the customers at Café Oberkampf and beyond. You might notice that the majority of layer cakes in this book use Italian meringue buttercream, because it's become my favorite. Very user-friendly once you get the hang of it, it's a good base frosting that can be flavored endlessly (think chocolate, caramel, and strawberry). But don't worry: There is a cake with a mascarpone whipped cream frosting (see page 76) that you'll love, too. And as a full-blooded Californian, I, of course, included one traditional American buttercream. You'll find it on my Vanilla Celebration Cake (page 200). I simply couldn't resist.

a few of my essential tools

a peek inside a baker's pantry

STAND MIXER. While this is a big investment, it really makes a baker's life much easier by allowing you to multitask in the kitchen. Note that most of the recipes in this book can be adapted to a hand mixer—they just may take a bit longer and require a bit more coordination.

SPRINGFORM CAKE PANS. I have a big collection of spring-form pans in different sizes, though I tend to use my 6-inch (15-cm) cake pans the most. Springform pans are my go-to for cake baking because I know the baked cakes will always easily release from the pan.

BUNDT PANS. Nordic Ware is constantly updating their Bundt pan designs, so pick your favorite and start planning your next Bundt cake. Here are some ideas: Banana Bundt Cake (page 48), Blueberry Lemon Bundt Cake (page 71), Cinnamon Swirl Bundt Cake (page 111), Persimmon Bundt Cake (page 130), and Blood Orange Mini Bundt Cakes (page 169).

FRIAND MOLDS. These oval aspic molds make a charming addition to your bakeware collection. Look for ones with an embossed star on the bottom. Use them to make Cherry Friands (page 68).

8- AND 9-INCH (20- AND 23-CM) TART PANS WITH REMOVABLE BOTTOMS. These are great for reducing stress, as they greatly reduce the chance of a broken tart when unmolding.

WIRE RACK: Perfect for cooling all your cakes and tarts on, and comes in handy when glazing a loaf or Bundt cake.

CAKE TURNTABLE. I love my Ateco cake turntable! It helps me achieve a smooth buttercream finish on all my layer cakes.

PASTRY TIPS AND DISPOSABLE PIPING BAGS. A basic set of piping tips will come in handy for cake decorating—I use my French star tip often. Disposable piping bags are wonderful and one less thing to clean up.

OFFSET PALETTE KNIFE. Invest in two different sizes— small and large—for applying buttercreams and ganache.

KITCHEN TORCH. A fun tool to have in your collection and essential for brûlée-ing a lemon meringue cake! (See page 159.)

chapter 1

le printemps

{ spring }

YOU'VE ALREADY HEARD me say it: Baking by season has taught me the delight of indulging in ingredients at their most delicious. But it's also schooled me in the art of anticipation—and the pleasure that exists in getting excited for what's to come.

No other season has prepped me for this lesson better than *le printemps* in Paris. Because, simply put, springtime here is a waiting game.

This surprised me at first, as I've always had one idea of this season lodged deep in my psyche: *April in Paris*, that Technicolor fantasy of the City of Light at its most majestic. Yet the reality? This part of year is not the Paris I'd pictured—at least, not all at once. Here, spring reveals its goodness layer by layer. I know now that it takes time to feel that first hint of warmth that allows you to remove a thick scarf or put away a pair of gloves. I wander through my neighborhood market on boulevard Richard-Lenoir with a patient smile, knowing that color and abundance will eventually make its way into my basket. And, as tough as it is, I know I'll need to hold on longer than I'd like for the ultimate "La Vie en Rose" moment—when the cherry blossoms explode into bloom, promising picnics sprinkled with a confetti of soft pink in places like the Palais-Royal, or, when we're adventurous, the Parc de Sceaux outside the city.

It'll all come in due time. But what's there for comfort as I wait for the baskets of cherries that will inevitably end up in the Pistachio Cherry Tea cake (page 45) or the gariguette strawberries and edible flowers that I'll use in a Marzipan Cake (page 59)? Chocolate and carbs.

After goûter, my favorite French-ism is lèche-vitrine, or window licking. (Yes, you read that right.) Despite its groan-inducing literal translation, lèche-vitrine is an expression for something divine: when you press your face close to the window of a shop in order to salivate over the beauty displayed inside . . . an experience that's never too few and far between here in France, especially around Pâques, the Easter holiday. This is when chocolate comes out in full force. The boutiques of chocolatiers around Paris—their windows worthy of a lick any season—all compete to craft the year's most lavish concoctions. In the windows, and along the counters, of names like La Maison du Chocolat, Patrick Roger, Debauve & Gallais—one of the city's oldest shops—and the newest kid on the chocolat block, Alain Ducasse, you'll find imaginative takes on chocolate eggs (with hidden candies inside); all manner of chocolate fish, lobsters, oysters, and shells, often filled with hazelnutty praliné; and chocolate versions of les cloches de Pâques, or Easter bells, rumored to fly from Rome to deliver treats to children on Easter morning. Even more over the top? The chocolate fest at Paris's ultraluxe palace hotels, where Michelin-starred pastry chefs try to outdo each other as they unveil their own Easter creations, often an outrageously elaborate egg made to be shared, if you're lucky, at an elegant goûter or afternoon tea with friends at one of the hotels' extravagant salons.

Afterward, if the weather's right, there's a chance you'll spot us rummaging at a nearby brocante, or local flea market. Spring is the time of year these weekend sales sprout back up after their winter hibernation, offering treasure hunters and antique collectors the chance to score deals on beautiful vintage finds. My favorite brocante happens to pop up near my home, the Brocante de la rue de Bretagne, where I'll scour the stalls for items to add to my collections of dessert plates and forks, platters and molds for cakes, servers (called pelles à tarte), and compotiers, old pedestaled bowls meant for fruit or compote that just happen to make excellent cake stands.

Carrying them home, I envision what will soon be served upon them: the Charlotte Rose topped with ripened red berries (page 33), a refreshing coconut and pineapple cake (see page 50), or perhaps a tarte à la rhubarb (see page 30). Because, just when I think I can't hold out much longer, the signs appear that the best part of the season has arrived. The warmth stays longer than three days in a row. The fuchsia magnolias begin to bud on the Champ-de-Mars, followed quickly by a cherry blossom bonanza. And, at my favorite markets in town, from the Marché Bastille to the Marché Saxe-Breteuil, I spot the biggest signals of all—the very first sightings of bright rhubarb and fat blackberries, of ripened apricots, cherries, and, yes (finally!), decadent strawberries. They'll be the basis for the baked goods that will soon be filling my oven, my kitchen, and the hands of friends joining me for a goûter beneath rows of pastel-petalled trees or simply gathered at my table, next to an open window, the afternoon breeze gently dancing through it.

And I believe we'll all agree the payoff was worth the wait.

treasure hunting at a paris flea market

Hunting for treasures at a fabulous flea market, or brocante, is one of my favorite pastimes, and here in France, there's even a verb for such an activity. Chiner *literally means to hunt for rare or old objects.* Le Marché aux Puces, *located in Saint-Ouen, just north of Paris, is said to be the oldest and largest in the world. Navigating its stalls, all stuffed with curiosities, can be overwhelming, so here are some tips from a seasoned flea market flâneur.*

1) Finding a flea market. Look for signs that pop up around the neighborhood, advertising an upcoming weekend brocante, or visit websites such as brocabrac. fr/75 for the most up-to-date information.

2) Arrive early, by 9:30 am, before the crowds, and you are likely to score that one-of-a-kind item before someone else spots it. I like to grab my coffee and croissant to go on mornings that I plan to be a serious shopper versus leisurely afternoon visits that are more for window shopping and photo taking.

3) Bring cash, as most vendors don't have credit card machines and—an added bonus—with cash in hand, you are likely to get a better deal. It never hurts to haggle a bit, though the prices at Saint-Ouen are more fixed than a more casual neighbor- hood flea market.

4) It's fun to throw a tea party with unique pieces on the table that your guests might want to know the story of, so I am always on the lookout for various dessert plates, teacups, saucers, and théières (teapots) to add to my collection. Having smaller, incomplete sets allows you to mix and match styles when hosting everything from an afternoon goûter to an elegant dinner party. Just as I like to bake seasonally, I find I bring

out certain seasonal styles and colors in my dessert ware as well—pastel teacups in summer and darker burgundy and gold cake plates in winter.

5) Look for old compotiers, or fruit bowls with pedestals. These make perfect cake stands and they come in a variety of styles and designs.

6) My most important brocante rule of all is if you see something you love, even if it's slightly cracked, peeling, or unpolished, you should nab it, since you might never come across it again. I love bringing home a well-spotted treasure. Even if I know it might not be an original, it's something that makes me smile.

tarte à la rhubarbe

Seeing all those pinkish hued stalks lined up in rows at the market stalls always signals spring for me. I don't remember eating much rhubarb before moving to France, but turns out I love it in baked tarts paired with vanilla ice cream. My husband is also a huge fan, and after lemon desserts, this is his second most-requested flavor. During spring, I'll make heaps of rhubarb compote to keep in the fridge and use on everything from Greek yogurt to crème anglaise. Frangipane lends a creamy richness to this tart and adds an almondy sweetness to contrast with the unsweetened rhubarb. The tart design was inspired by a flawless version created by a fellow baker/Instagram friend, Thida Bevington. I even enlisted the help of my photographer, Joann Pai, to piece together this pretty pattern. Feel free to arrange them in any design you like—the end result will be just as delicious! SERVES 6 TO 8

MAKE THE ALMOND TART DOUGH

1. In the bowl of a stand mixer fitted with the paddle attachment, combine the flour, powdered sugar, almond flour, butter, egg yolks, and salt on low until a dough forms. Do not overmix. When the dough comes together, shape into a disc and wrap in plastic wrap. Refrigerate the dough until firm, at least 1 hour.

2. Remove the almond tart dough from the refrigerator 30 minutes before you plan to roll it out. Preheat the oven to 400°F (200°C).

3. Transfer the dough to a lightly floured work surface and roll out to a large circle, about 12 inches (30 cm) in diameter. Carefully roll the dough around the rolling pin, brushing off any excess flour. Unroll the dough over a 9-inch (23-cm) tart pan with a removable bottom, gently tuck it into the pan, and trim any excess dough. Using a fork, poke tiny holes across the bottom of the tart shell. Line the tart shell with parchment paper and fill with pie weights to keep the dough from puffing up during baking. Bake for 10 minutes. Remove the tart shell from the oven and carefully remove the pie weights and parchment paper. Return the tart shell to the oven and bake for an additional 10 to 12 minutes, or until the center turns golden. Transfer the tart shell to a wire rack to cool completely.

FOR THE ALMOND TART DOUGH

1⅔ cups (210 g) all-purpose flour

⅔ cup (84 g) powdered sugar

¼ cup (28 g) almond flour

8 tablespoons (1 stick/113 g) unsalted butter, room temperature

2 large egg yolks, lightly beaten

Pinch of fine sea salt

FOR THE FRANGIPANE

¾ cup (150 g) granulated sugar

8 tablespoons (1 stick/113 g) unsalted butter, room temperature

2 large eggs, room temperature

1 cup (112 g) almond flour

1 teaspoon (5 ml) almond extract

1 tablespoon (8 g) all-purpose flour

FOR THE ASSEMBLY

3 to 4 large rhubarb stalks (about 18 ounces/510 g), cut into diagonal pieces

2 tablespoons (30 ml) acacia honey, warmed

Vanilla ice cream, for serving

CONTINUED FROM PAGE 30

MAKE THE FRANGIPANE FILLING

Meanwhile, in a medium bowl, whisk together the granulated sugar and butter until pale, about 4 minutes. Beat in the eggs until combined, then add the almond flour and almond extract and whisk until smooth. Add the flour and whisk once more until fully incorporated. Refrigerate until ready to use.

ASSEMBLY

1. Spread the frangipane filling evenly in the tart shell. Press the diagonal rhubarb pieces into the frangipane in an interlocking pattern. Bake for 30 to 35 minutes, or until the edges of the tart shell are golden brown. Transfer the tart to a wire rack to cool.

2. Brush the rhubarb with warm honey for a glossy finish and serve with vanilla ice cream.

charlotte rose

While a charlotte is said to be named after the only child of Britain's King George IV, Princess Charlotte, I've included it here in honor of my spunky New York niece Charlotte Rose. She was eleven when I first told her of my impending book deal, and upon hearing the news exclaimed, "Will there be a cake named after me?" A charlotte is essentially a trifle or cold dessert consisting of layers of sponge cake, cream, and fruit. In this case, biscuits line a mold, which is then filled with fruit purée custard. It's a French dessert that excels in any season, though I prefer the spring and summer iterations when berries are at their best. I consulted Charlotte during recipe development, and she approved of raspberries, though was less convinced of the rose syrup. I personally love the combination of raspberry and rose, which also pops up in my summertime tea cake (see page 82). It's a romantic flavor duo, but you can always swap the rose out for a vanilla simple syrup instead (see page 214). SERVES 6 TO 8

MAKE THE RASPBERRY BAVAROIS

1. In a small bowl, soak the gelatin sheets in ice-cold water; set aside.

In a food processor or blender, pulse the raspberries until smooth. Pour through a fine-mesh strainer set over a bowl and use a rubber spatula to press out as much juice as possible. Discard the solids.

2. In a small saucepan set over low heat, combine the milk and raspberry juice. Heat until just simmering. Meanwhile, whisk together the superfine sugar and egg yolks in a separate bowl until pale. Slowly pour the heated milk mixture over the egg mixture, whisking continuously. Pour the mixture back into the saucepan, set over medium-low heat, and cook until it just starts to thicken. Stir in the vanilla, then transfer the custard to a bowl.

3. Drain the gelatin sheets and add them to the custard, stirring until smooth. Cover the bowl with plastic wrap and refrigerate to set, about 1 hour.

MAKE THE ROSE SYRUP

Meanwhile, bring ½ cup (120 ml) water to a boil in a small saucepan set over medium heat. Add the granulated sugar and stir until it dissolves in the boiling water. Stir in the rose water, reduce the heat to low, cover the pan with a lid, and simmer for 15 minutes. Turn off the heat and allow the syrup to cool to room temperature. Transfer to a glass jar or other container, and store in the refrigerator until ready to use.

FOR THE RASPBERRY BAVAROIS

6 sheets gelatin

12½ ounces (355 g) raspberries

½ cup (120 ml) whole milk

½ cup (100 g) superfine sugar

3 large egg yolks

½ teaspoon (7.5 ml) pure vanilla extract

FOR THE ROSE SYRUP

¾ cup (150 g) granulated sugar

3 tablespoons (45 ml) rose water

FOR THE ASSEMBLY

24 to 26 ladyfingers

1¼ cups (300 ml) heavy cream, cold

3 cups (14 ounces/397 g) mixed berries

CONTINUED FROM PAGE 33

ASSEMBLY

1. Line an 8-inch (20-cm) round springform pan with parchment paper. If the ladyfingers are taller than the pan, trim the bottoms to fit the size of the pan. Dip the flat side of the ladyfingers in the rose syrup and line the pan with the rounded side of the biscuits facing out and the syrup-soaked side facing in. Once you've completed lining the sides of the pan, use the rest of the dipped biscuits to snugly fill the bottom of the pan.

2. In the bowl of a stand mixer fitted with the whisk attachment, whip the cold heavy cream until stiff peaks form. Gently fold the whipped cream into the raspberry custard using a rubber spatula. Spoon the bavarois into the ladyfinger-encrusted pan and refrigerate overnight to set.

3. To serve, carefully remove the springform pan, peel the parchment off the sides, and top with the mixed berries.

must-not-miss
spring experiences in paris

1) Practice the beautiful Japanese custom of hanami in Paris and seek out the city's cherry blossoms in some of my most loved spots: Champ-de-Mars at the Eiffel Tower, Parc Georges-Brassens, Parc des Buttes-Chaumont, and for the season's most splendid show, the famous grove at Parc de Sceaux, just a quick trip south via an RER train.

2) Judge for yourself the latest victor in the Grand Prix de la Baguette contest, held every April to award the best baguette in the city. In addition to a cash prize, the winning boulangerie receives the prestigious honor of supplying bread to the Élysée Palace—the French president's official residence—for one year.

3) Score a few vintage flea-market finds at a weekend brocante. (See page 28 for more details.) Look for signs to pop up around the neighborhood or visit websites such as brocabrac.fr/75 for the most updated information.

4) Take a charming day trip to the Château de Chantilly to see the glorious grounds as well as the second-largest collection of antique paintings in France after the Louvre. Afterward, be sure to taste the season's first strawberries paired with the best whipped cream in France!

5) See the fountains at Versailles. From April to October the Grandes Eaux Musicales brings the fountains to life set to music from the baroque period. The shows take place on Saturdays and Sundays as well as Tuesdays in the spring. Make sure to catch the grand finale at the Neptune fountain.

sakura financiers

In Japan, sakura, or cherry blossoms, are a potent symbol of renewal and, because they are so fleeting, a reminder to enjoy the beauty in life while you can. I wanted to include a nod to them in this chapter because I'm a fervent practitioner of hanami or simply "blossom viewing," where one appreciates the delicate blooms, often in the form of a picnic underneath a cloud of pink branches. What better way to celebrate the season than with a tiny matcha financier topped with a single preserved bloom? MAKES 12 FINANCIERS

MAKE THE FINANCIERS

1. Preheat the oven to 350°F (175°C). Grease and flour the financier molds or mini loaf pans; set aside.

2. Melt the butter in a small saucepan set over medium heat until lightly browned; set aside to cool.

3. In a large bowl, whisk together the flour, powdered sugar, ground almonds, matcha, and salt.

4. In a separate bowl, whisk the egg whites until they are light and frothy. Form a well in the flour mixture and pour the frothy egg whites in, along with the melted butter. Whisk just until a smooth, light batter forms.

5. Divide the batter evenly among the prepared molds, filling them about ⅔ full. Bake the financiers for 20 to 25 minutes, or until a cake tester inserted into the center comes out clean—the financiers will rise and crack on top. Transfer the financiers to a wire rack to cool for 5 minutes before removing from the molds to cool completely.

MAKE THE WHITE CHOCOLATE GLAZE

1. Place the white chocolate and heavy cream in a microwave-safe bowl and heat in 30-second increments, stirring occasionally, until melted. Add the powdered sugar and stir until well combined and smooth.

2. Place a sheet of parchment underneath the rack holding the cooled financiers. Pour the white chocolate glaze over the financiers, letting it drip down their sides. Place a salted cherry blossom in the center of each financier and allow the glaze to set at room temperature for about 15 minutes before serving.

FOR THE FINANCIERS

14 tablespoons (1¾ sticks/200 g) unsalted butter, plus additional for greasing

⅔ cup (85 g) all-purpose flour, plus additional for dusting

1⅔ cups (210 g) powdered sugar

⅔ cup (85 g) ground almonds

1 tablespoon (6 g) cooking-grade matcha powder

½ teaspoon (2.5 g) fine sea salt

5 large egg whites

FOR THE WHITE CHOCOLATE GLAZE

3 ounces (85 g) white chocolate, finely chopped

1½ tablespoons (23 ml) heavy cream

¼ cup (30 g) powdered sugar

12 salted cherry blossoms

A note on preserved cherry blossoms: Young blossoms are pickled just before full bloom with salt and plum vinegar over the course of six days. You can usually purchase them in small glass jars from Japanese grocery stores.

jasmine tea cakes

I adore sharing a pot of afternoon tea with friends, and while I have many tea moods, jasmine tea is one brew I could enjoy any time of day. With these cakes, I wanted to capture the aroma of a freshly brewed cup of Dragon Pearl Jasmine tea, tiny pearls of green tea laced with jasmine flowers that unfurl in hot water. Here, jasmine tea leaves get steeped in milk and then added to the batter to impart a light tea flavor, but the aroma comes from a single teaspoon of jasmine flower essence that perfumes all three cakes. Decorate these with edible pansies for a flower-filled afternoon. SERVES 6

MAKE THE TEA CAKES

1. In a small saucepan set over low heat, combine the milk and jasmine tea leaves. Bring the mixture to a simmer, stirring occasionally, about 4 minutes total. Turn off the heat and allow the tea to steep until cooled to room temperature.

2. Preheat the oven to 350°F (175°C). Grease and line three 6-inch (15-cm) round cake pans with parchment paper. Grease and flour the parchment paper. Set aside.

3. In the bowl of a stand mixer fitted with the paddle attachment, beat the granulated sugar and butter together on medium-high until pale and fluffy, about 4 minutes. With the mixer on low, add the eggs, one at a time, scraping down the bowl with a rubber spatula between additions. Add the jasmine flower oil and mix until combined.

4. In a medium bowl, whisk together the flour, baking powder, and salt.

5. Pour the milk through a fine-mesh strainer set over a small bowl; discard the tea leaves.

6. With the mixer on low, add the flour mixture in two additions, alternating with the milk. Mix until the batter just comes together.

7. Divide the batter evenly among the prepared pans. Bake for 30 to 35 minutes, or until a cake tester inserted into the center comes out clean and the tops are golden brown. Transfer the cakes to a wire rack to cool for 10 minutes before removing from the pans to cool completely.

FOR THE TEA CAKES

1 cup (240 ml) whole milk

2½ tablespoons (7.5 g) high-quality loose-leaf jasmine tea

14 tablespoons (1¾ sticks/200 g) unsalted butter, at room temperature, plus additional for greasing

2¼ cups (282 g) all-purpose flour, plus additional for dusting

1½ cups (300 g) granulated sugar

3 large eggs, room temperature

1 teaspoon (5 ml) culinary-grade jasmine flower oil

1½ teaspoons (6 g) baking powder

½ teaspoon (2.5 g) fine sea salt

FOR THE ITALIAN MERINGUE BUTTERCREAM

1 cup (200 g) granulated sugar

4 large egg whites

⅛ teaspoon (0.5 g) fine sea salt

2 cups (4 sticks/450 g) unsalted butter, room temperature

2 teaspoons (10 ml) pure vanilla extract

Food coloring gel, such as Wilton (optional)

FOR THE ASSEMBLY

Edible pansies (optional)

CONTINUED FROM PAGE 40

MAKE THE ITALIAN MERINGUE BUTTERCREAM

1. In a small saucepan set over high heat, combine the granulated sugar and ¼ cup (60 ml) water. Bring to a boil and continue cooking until the syrup reaches soft-ball stage, or 240°F (115°C) on a candy thermometer, 8 to 10 minutes.

2. Meanwhile, in the bowl of a stand mixer fitted with the whisk attachment, whisk the egg whites and salt on high until stiff peaks form.

3. Once the syrup has reached 240°F (115°C), carefully pour it into the egg white mixture in a slow steady stream with the mixer on low. Once all the syrup has been added, turn the mixer up to high and whisk until cool, about 5 minutes.

4. With the mixer set to medium-high, add the butter, 1 tablespoon (14 g) at a time, until fully combined. Once all the butter has been incorporated, add the vanilla and whip on high until light and fluffy, 4 to 5 minutes more.

5. If coloring your buttercream, separate out as much buttercream as you would like to color. You'll need about a quarter of the buttercream to cover each cake, which leaves a quarter for decorating. Gradually add color to your buttercream by dipping just the tip of a wooden toothpick into the food coloring gel and then swirling the color into the buttercream. Mix the buttercream to incorporate the color, gradually adding more food coloring gel until you get the shade you like.

ASSEMBLY

1. Using a serrated knife, level the cakes by trimming off the tops. Place the cakes on individual cake plates. Transfer about a quarter of the buttercream to a piping bag fitted with a medium French star pastry tip and set aside for decorating.

2. Using an offset palette knife, spread about a third of the remaining buttercream over the sides and tops of each cake. Use the buttercream in the piping bag to pipe rosettes or create a decorative border on each cake. Sprinkle the cakes with edible pansies, if using.

triple chocolate cake

The French art of lèche vitrine or window licking is most visible during the lead-up to Easter, when pastry chefs celebrate chocolate in all its glorious forms. Chocolate eggs, bunnies, and bells crowd the storefronts along the grand boulevards and avenues of the city, all hoping to be your goûter of the day. This recipe makes the perfect celebration cake for any chocolate lover in your life. It's a cocoa-infused creation filled with milk chocolate frosting and coated in rich bittersweet chocolate ganache. SERVES 8

MAKE THE CHOCOLATE CAKE

1. Preheat the oven to 350°F (175°C). Grease and line three 6-inch (15-cm) round cake pans with parchment paper. Grease and flour the parchment paper. Set aside.

2. In a large bowl, whisk together the flour, granulated sugar, cocoa powder, baking powder, baking soda, and salt.

3. While whisking, pour the hot coffee in a slow stream into the flour mixture. Add the oil and whisk until incorporated. Add the buttermilk and whisk until fully incorporated. Add the eggs, one at a time, mixing well after each addition, then add the vanilla and give the batter one last stir.

4. Divide the batter evenly among the prepared pans and bake for 30 to 35 minutes, or until a cake tester inserted into the center comes out clean—the cakes will rise and crack on top. Transfer the cakes to a wire rack to cool for 15 minutes before removing from the pans to cool completely.

MAKE THE GANACHE

1. Meanwhile, place the finely chopped bittersweet chocolate in a medium heatproof bowl.

2. In a small saucepan set over medium heat, bring the heavy cream just to a boil. Pour the hot cream over the chocolate and let stand for 2 minutes, then stir until the chocolate is melted and smooth. Allow to cool at room temperature until thickened to a spreadable consistency.

MAKE THE MILK CHOCOLATE BUTTERCREAM

1. Place the finely chopped milk chocolate in a microwave-safe bowl and heat in 30-second increments, stirring occasionally, until melted, or use the double-boiler method (see Note, on following page). Set aside to cool.

FOR THE CHOCOLATE CAKE

Unsalted butter, for greasing

2½ cups (315 g) all-purpose flour, plus additional for dusting

2 cups (400 g) granulated sugar

½ cup (50 g) Dutch-process cocoa powder, sifted

2 teaspoons (8 g) baking powder

2 teaspoons (8 g) baking soda

½ teaspoon (2.5 g) fine sea salt

1 cup (240 ml) strongly brewed coffee, hot

½ cup (120 ml) sunflower oil

1 cup (240 ml) buttermilk

2 large eggs, room temperature

1½ teaspoons (7.5 ml) pure vanilla extract

FOR THE GANACHE

18 ounces (510 g) 65% bittersweet chocolate, finely chopped

2¼ cups (540 ml) heavy cream

FOR THE MILK CHOCOLATE BUTTERCREAM

6 ounces (170 g) milk chocolate, finely chopped

14 tablespoons (1¾ sticks/200 g) unsalted butter, room temperature

3¼ cups (405 g) powdered sugar, sifted

6 tablespoons (36 g) Dutch-process cocoa powder

2 tablespoons (30 ml) heavy cream

CONTINUED FROM PAGE 43

2. In the bowl of a stand mixer fitted with the paddle attachment, beat the butter on medium-high until pale, 3 to 4 minutes. With the mixer on low, gradually add the powdered sugar, 1 cup (125 g) at a time. Once all the powdered sugar has been added, mix on medium-high until fluffy, about 3 minutes.

3. Add the melted chocolate, cocoa powder, and heavy cream, and mix until smooth, 3 to 4 minutes.

ASSEMBLY

1. Using a serrated knife, level the cakes by trimming off the tops. Spread a small spoonful of buttercream onto the center of the cake stand or plate to secure the cake, and place the first cake layer directly on top. Using an offset palette knife, spread about a third of the buttercream evenly on top of the cake, then place the second cake layer on top and repeat the process. Place the final cake layer on top. Spread the remaining butter-cream in a thin layer around the sides and top of the cake. Transfer the cake to the refrigerator to allow the crumb coat to set, about 20 minutes.

2. Using an offset palette knife, cover the sides and top of the cake with about ¾ of the ganache. Transfer the remaining ganache to a piping bag fitted with a medium French star pastry tip and pipe a ring of decorations on both the top and bottom edges of the cake.

Note: To melt chocolate in a double boiler, place the finely chopped pieces in a heatproof bowl set over a pan of simmering water and stir until melted.

pistachio cherry tea cake

One of my afternoon guilty pleasures is to cycle over to the Palais Royal gardens, pick up a pistachio financier or two from a nearby boulangerie, and enjoy it on a park bench with a coffee in hand. Spring is one of the best seasons to do so since it's when the magnolia trees lining the center of the garden begin to bloom. This tea cake is like a giant pistachio financier studded with in-season cherries, and its pretty pink glaze recalls the first flush of those pink petals at the garden I so love. I think tart cherries like Montmorency work particularly well with this cake, but raspberries work in a pinch, too. SERVES 12

MAKE THE PISTACHIO CAKE

1. Preheat the oven to 350°F (175°C). Grease and line an 8-x-4-inch (20-x-10-cm) loaf pan with parchment paper; set aside.

2. Set aside 1 tablespoon (8 g) of the flour. In a medium bowl, whisk together the remaining flour, the ground pistachios, baking powder, and salt; set aside.

3. In the bowl of a stand mixer fitted with the paddle attachment, beat the butter and granulated sugar together until combined, then add the sunflower oil and mix until pale and fluffy, about 3 minutes. With the mixer on low, add the eggs, one at a time, mixing well and scraping down the sides of the bowl with a rubber spatula after each addition. Add the vanilla and almond extracts and mix until just combined. Add the flour mixture in two additions, alternating with the milk, and mix until just combined.

4. In a small bowl, toss the cherry halves in the reserved 1 tablespoon (8 g) flour. Using a rubber spatula, gently fold the cherries into the batter.

5. Pour the batter into the prepared pan and bake for 45 to 55 minutes, or until a cake tester inserted into the center comes out clean and the cake is golden brown on top. Transfer the cake to a wire rack to cool for 15 minutes before removing from the pan to cool completely.

MAKE THE CHERRY GLAZE

Meanwhile, in a small bowl, whisk together the powdered sugar and cherry juice until well combined and smooth. Add more powdered sugar or cherry juice as needed to create a thick but pourable consistency.

FOR THE PISTACHIO CAKE

8 tablespoons (1 stick/113 g) unsalted butter, room temperature, plus additional for greasing

1¼ cups plus 3 tablespoons (181 g) all-purpose flour

½ cup (50 g) ground pistachios

2 teaspoons (8 g) baking powder

¼ teaspoon (1 g) fine sea salt

1 cup (200 g) granulated sugar

½ cup (120 ml) sunflower oil

2 large eggs, room temperature

1 teaspoon (5 ml) pure vanilla extract

½ teaspoon (2.5 ml) almond extract

⅔ cup (160 ml) whole milk, room temperature

1⅓ cups (5 ounces/140 g) cherries, pitted and halved

FOR THE CHERRY GLAZE

1 cup (125 g) powdered sugar, plus additional as needed

1 tablespoon (15 ml) cherry juice, plus additional as needed

FOR THE ASSEMBLY

1⅔ cups (6 ounces/170 g) cherries (about 10 to 12)

¼ cup (40 g) chopped pistachios

CONTINUED FROM PAGE 45

ASSEMBLY

1. Place a sheet of parchment paper underneath the rack holding the cooled cake. Starting at one end, slowly pour the glaze over the top of the cake, letting it drip down the sides, and going back and forth from one end to the other to completely cover the cake.

2. Arrange the cherries on top of the cake and sprinkle with the chopped pistachios. Allow the glaze to set at room temperature for about 15 minutes before serving.

banana bundt cake

I had to share one classic banana cake in my book, not only because it's such a crowd-pleaser but also because it is the signature cake of my aunt Penelope, who, in my eyes, is our family's baking superstar. I have very fond memories of sharing her famous banana nut bread, still warm from the oven, whenever we'd visit her house, which was often, thanks to that legendary loaf. Her version calls for toasted walnuts, but I prefer pecans—sorry, Aunt Penny! Banana cake often tastes better the day after it's baked. I recommend eating a toasted slice with salted butter whenever possible.

SERVES 12

MAKE THE BANANA CAKE

1. Preheat the oven to 350°F (175°C). Grease and flour a 10- to 12-cup (2.4- to 2.8-L) Bundt pan or use baking spray; set aside.

2. In a medium bowl, whisk together the flour, cinnamon, baking powder, baking soda, and salt.

3. In the bowl of a stand mixer fitted with the paddle attachment, beat the butter and dark brown sugar together on medium-high until pale and fluffy, about 4 minutes. With the mixer on low, add the eggs, one at a time, mixing well after each addition. Add the vanilla and mix until just combined.

4. Using a wooden spoon, stir in the mashed bananas until combined. Add the flour in two additions, alternating with the crème fraîche, and stir with a wooden spoon just until there is no flour visible. Stir in the nuts, if using.

5. Pour the batter into the prepared pan and bake for 45 to 50 minutes, or until a cake tester inserted into the center comes out clean and the cake is golden brown. Transfer the cake to a wire rack to cool for 15 minutes before carefully removing from the pan to cool completely.

MAKE THE VANILLA GLAZE

1. Meanwhile, in a medium bowl, whisk together the powdered sugar, milk, and vanilla until well combined and smooth. Add more powdered sugar or milk as needed to create a thick but pourable glaze.

2. Place a sheet of parchment paper underneath the rack holding the cooled cake. Slowly pour the glaze over the top of the Bundt, allowing it to drip down the sides. Allow the glaze to set at room temperature for about 15 minutes before serving.

FOR THE BANANA CAKE

8 tablespoons (1 stick/113 g) unsalted butter, room temperature, plus additional for greasing

2 cups (250 g) all-purpose flour, plus additional for dusting

1½ teaspoons (3 g) ground cinnamon

1 teaspoon (4 g) baking powder

1 teaspoon (4 g) baking soda

½ teaspoon (2.5 g) fine sea salt

1 cup (220 g) firmly packed dark brown sugar

2 large eggs, room temperature

1 teaspoon (5 ml) pure vanilla extract

4 overripe bananas, mashed

1 cup (225 g) crème fraîche

½ cup (60 g) chopped pecans, toasted (optional)

FOR THE VANILLA GLAZE

2½ cups (310 g) powdered sugar, plus additional as needed

3 tablespoons (45 ml) whole milk, plus additional as needed

1 teaspoon (5 ml) pure vanilla extract

coconut & pineapple cake

All the textures in this spring cake make me smile. Shredded coconut, fluffy cake, and smooth pineapple curd come together in a tropical trifecta. With a cheerful and brightly flavored pineapple curd, combined with cake layers sweetened with coconut cream, it's a nice alternative to a chocolate dessert at Eastertime. It's also a great cake to bake during that shoulder season in early spring, while you are waiting for all the fresh fruit to appear at the market stalls. Just make sure to use canned pineapple juice, not the variety of overly sweetened fruit beverages, which do not thicken properly. The extra pineapple curd in this recipe makes a great filling for a tart or an extravagant topping on your morning brioche. It's also important to use coconut cream rather than coconut milk. It has a higher fat content, which means less water and more coconut, resulting in a thicker consistency. It keeps, covered in the fridge, for up to ten days.

SERVES 12

MAKE THE COCONUT CAKE

1. Preheat the oven to 350°F (175°C). Grease and line two 9-inch (23-cm) round cake pans with parchment paper. Grease and flour the parchment paper. Set aside.

2. In a medium bowl, whisk together the milk, coconut cream, eggs, egg whites, and vanilla; set aside.

3. In the bowl of a stand mixer fitted with the paddle attachment, combine the flour, granulated sugar, baking powder, and salt. Mix on low until combined.

4. With the mixer on low, add the softened butter, 1 tablespoon (14 g) at a time, mixing well after each addition. Once all the butter has been added, slowly add half of the milk mixture and mix on medium-high until smooth. Turn the mixer back to low, add the remaining milk mixture, and mix until just combined. Using a rubber spatula, give the batter one final mix.

5. Divide the batter evenly between the prepared pans. Bake for 30 to 35 minutes, or until a cake tester inserted into the centers comes out clean and the cakes are golden brown. Transfer the cakes to a wire rack to cool for 10 minutes before removing from the pans to cool completely.

MAKE THE PINEAPPLE CURD

Meanwhile, in a medium saucepan off the heat, combine the pineapple juice, granulated sugar, eggs, egg yolks, and cornstarch. Whisk until

FOR THE COCONUT CAKE

1½ cups (3 sticks/336 g) unsalted butter, room temperature, plus additional for greasing

4¾ cups (594 g) all-purpose flour, plus additional for dusting

1½ cups plus 1 tablespoon (375 ml) whole milk

¾ cup (180 ml) coconut cream

2 large eggs, room temperature

4 large egg whites, room temperature

1 teaspoon (5 ml) pure vanilla extract

2 cups (400 g) granulated sugar

1 tablespoon (12 g) baking powder

½ teaspoon (2.5 g) fine sea salt

FOR THE PINEAPPLE CURD

½ cup (120 ml) canned pineapple juice

½ cup (100 g) granulated sugar

2 large eggs

2 large egg yolks

2 tablespoons (16 g) cornstarch

2 tablespoons (28 g) unsalted butter, cubed

CONTINUED FROM PAGE 50

smooth, then set over medium-low heat and cook, stirring constantly with a wooden spoon, until thickened, about 10 minutes. Take the pan off the heat. Stir in the butter, one cube at a time, and stir until the curd is velvety and uniform in texture. Transfer to a glass bowl and cover with plastic wrap, pressing it directly on the surface of the curd to prevent a skin forming. Refrigerate until cold.

MAKE THE COCONUT ITALIAN MERINGUE BUTTERCREAM

1. Combine the granulated sugar and ¼ cup (60 ml) water in a small saucepan set over high heat. Bring to a boil and continue cooking until the syrup reaches soft-ball stage, or 240°F (115°C) on a candy thermometer, 8 to 10 minutes.

2. Meanwhile, in the bowl of a stand mixer fitted with the whisk attachment, whisk the egg whites and salt on high until stiff peaks form.

3. Once the syrup has reached 240°F (115°C), carefully pour it into the egg white mixture in a slow steady stream with the mixer on low. Once all the syrup has been added, turn the mixer up to high and whisk until cool, about 5 minutes.

4. With the mixer set to medium-high, add the butter, 1 tablespoon (14 g) at a time, until fully combined. Once all the butter has been added, add the coconut cream and vanilla and whip on high until light and fluffy, 4 to 5 minutes more.

ASSEMBLY

1. Using a serrated knife, level the cakes by trimming off the tops. Place one cake round on a cake plate or stand. Transfer 2 large spoonfuls of the buttercream to a piping bag fitted with a medium round pastry tip and pipe a circle around the top outer edge of the cake. Fill the circle with about 5 tablespoons (75 ml) of the cold pineapple curd, spreading it to evenly cover the top of the cake. Place the other cake round on top and use an offset palette knife to spread a thin layer of buttercream over the sides and top of the cake. Transfer the cake to the refrigerator to allow the crumb coat to set, about 20 minutes.

2. Cover the sides and top of the cake with the remaining buttercream.

3. Sprinkle shredded coconut on top of the cake then gently press coconut up and down the sides of the cake to cover completely. Decorate with dried pineapple flowers, if using.

Note: Dried pineapple flowers are available at most organic grocery stores.

FOR THE COCONUT ITALIAN MERINGUE BUTTERCREAM

1 cup (200 g) granulated sugar

4 large egg whites

⅛ teaspoon (0.5 g) fine sea salt

2 cups (4 sticks/450 g) unsalted butter, room temperature

2 tablespoons (30 ml) coconut cream

2 teaspoons (10 ml) pure vanilla extract

FOR THE ASSEMBLY

2 cups (160 g) unsweetened shredded coconut

Dried pineapple flowers (optional)

marble tea cake

Marble is always a great option when you can't decide between chocolate or vanilla cake. This recipe is partly inspired by a version I had at the historic Dalloyau pâtisserie on rue du Faubourg Saint-Honoré. I loved the addition of their crunchy almond glaze, which reminded me of another iconic chocolate, vanilla, and almond combination, Magnum ice cream bars. It's equally delicious served without the glaze in case you want a simpler snacking cake to get you through the week. SERVES 12

MAKE THE CAKE

1. Preheat the oven to 350°F (175°C). Grease and line a 10-x-5-inch (25-x-12.5-cm) loaf pan with parchment paper; set aside.

2. Melt the butter in a small saucepan set over low heat; set aside.

3. In a medium bowl, whisk together the flour, baking powder, and salt; set aside.

4. In the bowl of a stand mixer fitted with the whisk attachment, whisk the granulated sugar and eggs on high until thick and pale, about 4 minutes. Turn the mixer down to low then add the melted butter, yogurt, and vanilla and mix until combined. Gradually add the flour mixture in three additions and mix until just combined.

5. Transfer half of the batter to a separate bowl, then sift the cocoa powder over that half of the batter and use a rubber spatula to mix until combined. Starting and ending with vanilla batter, pour thin, alternating layers of the vanilla and chocolate batter into the prepared pan. To make the marble swirl, use the point of a butter knife to draw a zigzag pattern through the batter. Bake for 45 to 50 minutes, or until a cake tester inserted into the center comes out clean and the top of the cake is golden brown. Transfer the cake to a wire rack to cool for 10 minutes before removing from the pan to cool completely.

MAKE THE CHOCOLATE GLAZE

1. Preheat the oven to 300°F (150°C). Line a baking tray with parchment paper. Add the chopped hazelnuts and roast for 10 to 15 minutes, or until fragrant. Set aside to cool.

2. Place the finely chopped milk chocolate in a microwave-safe bowl and heat in 30-second increments, stirring occasionally, until melted, or use the double-boiler method (see Note, page 44). Stir in the grapeseed oil and mix until smooth, then stir in the roasted hazelnuts. Keep warm.

FOR THE CAKE

9 tablespoons (125 g) unsalted butter, plus additional for greasing

2 cups (250 g) all-purpose flour

2 teaspoons (8 g) baking powder

¼ teaspoon (1 g) fine sea salt

1 cup (200 g) granulated sugar

3 large eggs, room temperature

½ cup (120 g) plain whole milk Greek yogurt

1 teaspoon (5 ml) pure vanilla extract

2 tablespoons plus 1 teaspoon (14 g) Dutch-process cocoa powder

FOR THE CHOCOLATE GLAZE

¼ cup (29 g) chopped hazelnuts

8 ounces (225 g) milk chocolate, finely chopped

2½ tablespoons (38 ml) grapeseed oil

CONTINUED FROM PAGE 53

ASSEMBLY

1. Place a sheet of parchment paper underneath the rack holding the cooled cake.

2. Starting at one end, slowly pour the warm glaze over the top of the cake, going back and forth from one end to the other and using an offset palette knife as needed to gently push the glaze so it completely covers the top and sides of the cake. Let the glaze set at room temperature for 45 minutes to 1 hour before serving.

blooms in my basket: le printemps

As it transitions from winter's lingering chill to warmer, later-season days, spring offers a steady stream of cheerful, sunny blooms at local markets that make beautiful at-home bouquets.

TULIPS. With so many varieties to choose from, you can select a different tulip each week throughout most of the season. My favorite? Parrot tulips, with their flamboyant fringe. I tend to favor the "color blocking" technique of grouping flowers of the same color with different size blooms and textures—it creates a simple bouquet, but it makes a striking statement.

HYACINTHS. These cheery flowers are one of the earliest signs that spring has come to Paris. Because of their gorgeously rich fragrance, I often place them in my kitchen.

LILIES OF THE VALLEY. On May 1, it's customary in France to offer *muguet*, or lily of the valley, to loved ones for luck—a gesture dating back to the 1560 court of King Charles IX. In fact, you see people selling muguet on the streets on the date; the government allows their tax-free sale on "May Day" to keep the tradition going.

POPPIES. What's friendlier than a perky poppy? I like to hunt for the larger, hardier Icelandic variety at my local fleuriste, as they offer so much elegance and drama when they finally unfurl.

EDIBLE FLOWERS. I often decorate my spring cakes with safe-to-eat flowers like nasturtiums and pansies—tiny, delicate blooms that come in deep purples, yellows, whites, and pinks. They're pricey, but they're not difficult to find in Paris at some stores and épiceries. If you don't have edible flowers at a market or florist near you, look to order them fresh online.

marzipan cake

This marzipan cake is Norwegian in origin, and is typically simple and fresh. I know marzipan can be a bit divisive, but it's absolutely essential here as it holds together all that whipped cream balanced delicately on top of the light-as-air sponge cake. Decorate with seasonal blooms like cherry blossoms and ripe strawberries or raspberries for a lovely afternoon teatime. SERVES 8 TO 10

MAKE THE CAKE

1. Preheat the oven to 325°F (165°C). Line an 8-inch (20-cm) round springform pan with parchment paper; set aside.

2. In the bowl of a stand mixer fitted with the whisk attachment, beat the eggs on high for 1 minute and then gradually add the granulated sugar and continue beating on high until thick and fluffy, about 6 minutes.

3. In a medium bowl, whisk together the flour and baking powder. Gently fold the flour mixture into the egg mixture in three additions, being careful not to deflate the batter. Add the almond extract and mix just to incorporate.

4. Pour the batter into the prepared pan and bake for 30 to 35 minutes, or until a cake tester inserted into the center comes out clean and the cake is golden brown. Transfer the cake to a wire rack to cool completely then remove from the pan.

MAKE THE WHIPPED CREAM

In the bowl of a stand mixer fitted with the whisk attachment, combine the heavy cream, powdered sugar, and vanilla and whip on high until stiff peaks form, 3 to 5 minutes.

ASSEMBLY

1. Use a large serrated knife to cut the cake into two thin layers. Place the first cake layer on a cake plate or stand. Using an offset palette knife, spread the strawberry jam over the top of the cake, leaving a 1-inch (2.5-cm) border around the edge. Spoon about a third of the whipped cream on top of the jam layer and use a clean offset palette knife to cover the entire top of the cake. Place the second cake layer on top and use the remaining whipped cream to cover the sides and top of the cake.

2. Roll out the marzipan to a ¼ inch (6 mm) thickness on a surface dusted lightly with powdered sugar. Trim any excess marzipan and decorate with cherry blossoms and strawberries. Refrigerate until ready to serve.

FOR THE CAKE

4 large eggs, room temperature

½ cup plus 2 tablespoons (125 g) granulated sugar

1 cup (125 g) all-purpose flour

1 teaspoon (4 g) baking powder

½ teaspoon (2.5 ml) almond extract

FOR THE WHIPPED CREAM

3 cups (720 ml) heavy cream, cold

½ cup (60 g) powdered sugar

1 teaspoon (5 ml) pure vanilla extract

FOR THE ASSEMBLY

¼ cup (80 g) seedless strawberry jam

1 pound (450 g) marzipan

Powdered sugar, for dusting

6 to 7 cherry blossom blooms (from 1 branch)

1 cup (5 ounces/144 g) strawberries, preferably gariguette or other small variety

shop a market like a parisian

Make the most of a trip to the marché with these tips.

1) Know when the open-air market opens in your neighborhood with a quick look online (parisinfo.com is often a smart choice). Neighborhoods usually have markets twice per week, beginning generally at 8 am and ending around 1 pm.

2) Go first thing in the morning for the best selection, or hit the end of the market if you'd prefer to score deals on super ripe and ready-to-go produce.

3) Bring a basket or favorite canvas bag; vendors don't often have bags to supply for you.

4) Stash some cash in your wallet as a backup to credit cards, as some vendors won't have card machines handy.

5) Always greet a vendor with a friendly "bonjour" when you approach their stall.

6) Don't assume you'll be picking your own produce. Tell the vendor what you're looking for (or just point!) and they'll either select the item for you or give you the go-ahead to choose your own.

7) If your French is up to it, it's also smart to tell a vendor how you're using something—an apple to slice into a bowl of yogurt for breakfast vs. an apple to bake in a tart, for example— as he or she will be able to help you find your best fit.

chapter 2

l'été

{ summer }

SUMMERTIME IN PARIS is a complete crowd-pleaser. With its sunny outlook and calendar crammed with celebrations, this is the season everyone lives for. It kicks off with June's Fête de la Musique, where bands take over entire neighborhoods for raucous all-night concerts (with my sympathies to the residents of those apartments). It continues with festive evenings at chateaux grounds around Paris—like the dreamy candlelit Château de Vaux-le-Vicomte—and culminates in the granddaddy of all parties, Bastille Day, where you can pop a cork with the throngs on the Champ-de-Mars or simply pop over to a nearby bridge to catch the wow-worthy fireworks lighting up the night of July 14.

The thing worth noting here? All events occur in the one place Parisians want to be in the summer: outdoors. Due to its small apartment sizes, stifling indoor temps (sans A/C), and a generous sun that doesn't set until past 10 pm, this city, more than any other, likes to shift its living outside during the warm months. Residents rush to fill the streets, pack the parks, and dine on both café terraces and their own home balconies, where even those with the tiniest of perches will ensure every meal is enjoyed alfresco, no matter how tight the squeeze.

And there's nowhere better to witness this commitment to the open-air than the heart of the season's activity . . . the river.

For me, Seine-side living is a hallmark of summer. Its cool breezes draw Parisians like magnets, and not only for its now-famous Paris Plages, those temporary beaches with lazy lounge chairs, umbrellas, and mist machines for those who can't steal away to Saint-Tropez. For most of us, taking to the Seine is about grabbing a group of friends and a bottle of rosé to go bask on the banks and watch the boats cruising by. It's an ideal spot for an easy goûter—pack your own Lavender Honey Madeleines (page 93) or stop at Aux Merveilleux de Fred for a pain au lait or cramique chocolat—or for a picnic with cheeses and fruit (bonus points for those bringing baskets, blankets, and real stemware). Like me, most Parisians have their favorite spots, whether a tree-filled hideaway just around the Île Saint-Louis or a more dramatic site across from the Musée d'Orsay next to the Tuileries, where you can lounge with an unmatched view of the Eiffel Tower as its diamond lights sparkle late into the season's long, hazy evenings.

It's a Parisian party that doesn't seem to end. Until it does. Because those crowds by the river? They dissipate eventually, as do the crowds everywhere else. And between us, the transformation of the city into a sleepy village along the Seine is the most pleasing part of summer.

When we first relocated here, I started noticing hand-scribbled signs going up in the windows of stores and restaurants sometime around mid-July. "Back at the end of the summer holidays," they'd read in their charming French cursive. "Bonnes vacances . . . have a nice time," others exclaimed. I'd soon learn that these were the equivalent of old-timey "Gone Fishin'" notices. Because the other place Parisians want to be in summertime other than the outdoors?

On vacation.

In what may be a surprising turn of events for first-time visitors (as it certainly was for this California boy), Paris empties out toward the middle of the summer as les vacances beckon its citizens to more coastal climes. And I don't mean just your everyday residents. I am talking entire boutiques, cafés, restaurants, and coffee shops—closed for a month. This leaves behind a vacant city that's more akin to a quiet village than the bustling metropolis it is otherwise. Most people see this as the time to escape. But I view it as an opportunity to see things in a new way—and I stay. With the traffic gone and streets silent, this town becomes a playground, where most days you'll find me riding my bike almost anywhere. It's the one part of the year I feel brave enough to cycle far from home; I sometimes have whole boulevards and avenues to myself. A cleared-out Paris opens itself up to me, showing its simpler side, if only for a brief period of time.

It reminds me much of my philosophy for summertime baking, in fact: to scale back and let the brightness of the season shine through. It's an emphasis on minimalism that's only enhanced by the offerings at our summer markets. The fruits stacked high in their stalls entice like nothing else—the cherries, berries, and varieties of strawberries at peak sweetness; stone fruit like apricots and white peaches that bewitch at first bite; tantalizing mango; surprising and versatile rhubarb; aptly named passion fruit. And while I will use these summery ingredients in the occasional layer cake like my Fraisier Layer Cake (page 75)—it is a party season and there's always cause for buttercream—it's my lighter, simpler recipes like Tarte aux Fraises (page 73), and Cherry Friands (page 68) that make it into heavy rotation. They're delightful as an everyday treat, a dessert to share when everyone's still in town, or for a solo snack by the Seine, as you indulge in a moment's respite from the heat and discover a little burst of seasonal beauty on your own. And that's always something to celebrate.

cherry friands

I often visit the storied aisles of Paris's oldest cookware shop, E.Dehillerin, to gawk at the shiny copper pots and pans, cake tins, and various other kitchen essentials they've been selling to inhabitants of and visitors to the City of Light since 1820. It was on one such visit that I spied a stack of the most charming steel tin oval molds with an embossed star pattern on top. I discovered later that they were aspic molds for jelly, but I immediately knew I'd use them to make perfect little afternoon teatime cakes. Turns out, a French chef working in Australia had already thought to do the same and called them "friands." Friands—almond-rich cakes inspired by the financier but baked in aspic molds to give them their signature oval shape—pair perfectly with various seasonal fruits. I'll admit, though, that I'm most fond of their sweet almond flavor combined with tart summertime cherries. (If you aren't able to find these particular molds, a muffin tin will suffice.) MAKES 8 FRIANDS

14 tablespoons (1¾ sticks/200 g) unsalted butter, plus additional for greasing

⅔ cup (85 g) all-purpose flour, plus additional for dusting

1⅔ cups (210 g) powdered sugar, plus additional for dusting

⅔ cup (85 g) ground almonds

½ teaspoon (2.5 g) fine sea salt

5 large egg whites

Grated zest of 1 lemon

8 cherries, pitted and halved, plus additional for serving

1. Preheat the oven to 350°F (175°C). Grease and flour the friand molds (or a standard 12-cup muffin tin); set aside.

2. Melt the butter in a small saucepan set over medium heat; set aside to cool.

3. In a large bowl, sift together the flour and powdered sugar. Stir in the ground almonds and salt.

4. In a medium bowl, whisk the egg whites until light and frothy. Form a well in the flour mixture and pour the frothy egg whites in, along with the lemon zest and melted butter. Stir until a light batter forms.

5. Divide the batter evenly among the prepared molds, filling them about ⅔ full. Place 2 cherry halves into each mold and bake for 20 to 25 minutes, or until a cake tester inserted into the centers comes out clean and the friands are golden brown. Transfer the cakes to a wire rack to cool for 5 to 6 minutes before removing from the molds to cool completely. Serve dusted with powdered sugar and additional cherries alongside.

blueberry lemon bundt cake

In the first few weeks of June, I start pestering the vendors at my local épicerie on rue de Bretagne about when we might expect myrtilles sauvages (wild blueberries) to come in. The tiny blueberries—usually from regions in the east of France like Vosges and Ardèche—are small, but pack an intense blueberry flavor. I call this a breakfast or brunch Bundt since it's bursting with both blueberries and buttermilk. SERVES 12

MAKE THE BLUEBERRY LEMON CAKE

1. Preheat the oven to 350°F (175°C). Grease and flour a 10- to 12-cup (2.4- to 2.8-L) Bundt pan or use baking spray; set aside.

2. Set aside 1 tablespoon (8 g) of the flour. Place the remaining flour in a medium bowl. Add the baking powder, baking soda, and salt and whisk to combine; set aside.

3. In a small bowl, whisk together the buttermilk, lemon zest, lemon juice, and vanilla; set aside.

4. In the bowl of a stand mixer fitted with the paddle attachment, beat the butter and granulated sugar together on medium-high until pale and fluffy, about 4 minutes. With the mixer on low, add the eggs, one at a time, and mix well, scraping down the sides of the bowl with a rubber spatula between additions. Add the flour mixture in three additions, alternating with the buttermilk mixture, and mix until just combined.

5. In a small bowl, toss the blueberries in the reserved 1 tablespoon (8 g) flour. Gently fold the blueberries into the batter using a rubber spatula.

6. Pour the batter into the prepared pan and bake for 55 to 60 minutes, or until a cake tester inserted into the center comes out clean and the cake is golden brown. Transfer the cake to a wire rack to cool for 10 minutes before carefully removing from the pan to cool completely.

MAKE THE LEMON GLAZE

1. Meanwhile, in a medium bowl, whisk together the powdered sugar, milk, and lemon juice until well combined and smooth. Add more powdered sugar or milk as needed to create a thick but pourable glaze.

2. Place a sheet of parchment paper underneath the rack holding the cooled cake. Pour the glaze over the top of the cake, letting it drip down the sides.

3. Decorate with a crown of dark summer berries. Allow the glaze to set at room temperature for about 15 minutes before serving.

FOR THE BLUEBERRY LEMON CAKE

1 cup (2 sticks/225 g) unsalted butter, room temperature, plus additional for greasing

2¾ cups plus 1 tablespoon (352 g) all-purpose flour, plus additional for dusting

1½ teaspoons (6 g) baking powder

¼ teaspoon (1 g) baking soda

¼ teaspoon (1 g) fine sea salt

1 cup (240 ml) buttermilk

2 tablespoons (12 g) grated lemon zest (from 2 lemons)

2 tablespoons (30 ml) freshly squeezed lemon juice

1½ teaspoons (7.5 ml) pure vanilla extract

2 cups (400 g) granulated sugar

4 large eggs, room temperature

2 cups (10 ounces/280 g) fresh blueberries, ideally wild

FOR THE LEMON GLAZE

1⅓ cups (167 g) powdered sugar, plus additional as needed

2 tablespoons (30 ml) whole milk, plus additional as needed

1 tablespoon (15 ml) freshly squeezed lemon juice

1½ cups (8 ounces/225 g) dark summer berries, such as blueberries and blackberries

tarte aux fraises

During spring and summer, you'll find this classic strawberry tart in almost every pastry case in Paris. It's a dessert that beautifully celebrates the season, since the strawberries are fresh and at their peak. The diplomat cream is really just a fancy name for pastry cream with whipped cream folded in—the perfect companion to a summertime tart topped with ripe berries. SERVES 6

MAKE THE PÂTE SABLÉE

1. In a medium bowl, whisk together the flour, powdered sugar, and salt. Add the cubed butter and rub it into the flour mixture with your fingers until it resembles coarse sand. Add the egg and use a fork to mix the dough until it just comes together and there are no dry bits left. Using your hands, form the dough into a ball. Wrap the dough in plastic wrap and refrigerate until firm, at least 1 hour.

2. Remove the pâte sablée from the refrigerator 30 minutes before you plan to roll it out. Grease and flour a 9-inch (23-cm) tart pan with a removable bottom.

3. Transfer the dough to a lightly floured work surface and roll out to a large circle, about 12 inches (30 cm) in diameter. Carefully roll the dough around the rolling pin, brushing off any excess flour. Unroll the dough over the prepared pan, gently tuck it into the pan, and trim any excess dough. Using a fork, poke tiny holes across the bottom of the tart shell. Return to the refrigerator to chill for 20 minutes.

4. Preheat the oven to 350°F (175°C). Line the tart shell with parchment paper and fill with pie weights to keep the dough from puffing up during baking. Bake for 20 minutes. Remove the tart shell from the oven and carefully remove the pie weights and parchment paper. Return the tart shell to the oven and bake for an additional 10 minutes, or until the center turns golden. Transfer the tart shell to a wire rack to cool completely.

MAKE THE DIPLOMAT CREAM

1. Meanwhile, in a medium saucepan set over medium heat, combine 2 cups (480 ml) of the heavy cream and ⅓ cup (68 g) of the granulated sugar. Using the tip of a sharp knife, scrape the seeds from the ½ vanilla bean into the pan and bring to a gentle boil, stirring occasionally.

FOR THE PÂTE SABLÉE

2 cups (250 g) all-purpose flour, plus additional for dusting

½ cup (60 g) powdered sugar

Pinch of fine sea salt

9 tablespoons (125 g) unsalted butter, cold and cubed, plus additional for greasing

1 large egg

FOR THE DIPLOMAT CREAM

4 cups (960 ml) heavy cream, cold

⅓ cup (68 g) plus ¼ cup (50 g) granulated sugar

½ vanilla bean, split lengthwise

½ cup (64 g) cornstarch

5 large egg yolks

¼ cup (½ stick/56 g) unsalted butter, room temperature

FOR THE ASSEMBLY

5 cups (26 ounces/737 g) fresh strawberries, hulled and cut in half

Powdered sugar, for dusting

Note: 1 whole vanilla bean is equal to 1 tablespoon (15 ml) pure vanilla extract. Feel free to substitute in the recipe if you don't have pods in your pantry.

CONTINUED FROM PAGE 73

2. Meanwhile, in a medium bowl, whisk together the cornstarch, egg yolks, and the remaining ¼ cup (50 g) granulated sugar.

3. Once the cream has reached a gentle boil, pour half of it into the egg yolk mixture, whisking continuously. Return the egg yolk mixture to the saucepan set over medium heat and whisk vigorously until thickened, 1 to 2 minutes. Remove from the heat, add the butter, 1 tablespoon (14 g) at a time, and whisk until smooth. Transfer the pastry cream to a bowl and cover with plastic wrap, pressing it directly onto the surface of the cream to prevent a skin forming. Refrigerate until set, about 2 hours.

4. In the bowl of a stand mixer fitted with the whisk attachment, whip the remaining 2 cups (480 ml) heavy cream on high until stiff peaks form. Remove the set pastry cream from the refrigerator and fold a few spoonfuls into the freshly whipped cream with a rubber spatula. Gently fold the rest of the pastry cream into the whipped cream until smooth.

ASSEMBLY

1. Place the cooled tart shell on a serving platter. Spread the diplomat cream evenly inside the shell and arrange the strawberry halves, cut side down, in a circular pattern. Refrigerate until ready to serve.

2. Dust with powdered sugar just before serving.

fraisier layer cake

At the start of this sunny season, I journey across the Seine to make my way to Mori Yoshida, a small pastry shop on avenue de Breteuil in the shadow of Les Invalides. It's there where you'll find one of Paris's best fraisiers, a traditional cake composed of layers of kirsch-soaked genoise—a light-as-air sponge cake—creme patisserie, marzipan, and deliciously fresh strawberries. Here in France, we have several varieties of strawberries available during the summer months: gariguette, mara des bois, anaïs, and the tiny yet flavor-intense fraise des bois, or wild forest strawberry. In this recipe, any type of strawberry will lend its own unique flavor, but what is most important is that your strawberries are ripe and in season. In this version, I layer strawberry pastry cream between white cake layers, and wrap everything in a mascarpone whipped cream frosting. This cake is an ode to the sweet beginning of summertime! SERVES 12

MAKE THE STRAWBERRY PASTRY CREAM

1. In a medium saucepan set over medium heat, combine the heavy cream, ⅓ cup (68 g) of the granulated sugar, and salt and bring to a gentle boil, stirring occasionally.

2. Meanwhile, in a medium bowl, whisk together the egg yolks, cornstarch, and the remaining ¼ cup (50 g) granulated sugar. Once the cream has reached a gentle boil, pour half of it into the egg yolk mixture, whisking continuously. Once the egg mixture has been tempered, add it back to the saucepan with the remaining hot cream, whisking continuously. Turn the heat up to medium-high and continue to whisk the entire mixture until it begins to thicken, about 2 minutes. Remove from the heat and whisk in the jam, butter, and vanilla.

3. Transfer the pastry cream to a bowl and cover with plastic wrap, pressing it directly onto the surface of the cream to prevent a skin forming. Refrigerate to set, at least 2 hours or overnight.

MAKE THE STRAWBERRY SYRUP

1. Meanwhile, in a food processor or blender, pulse the strawberries until smooth. Pour through a fine-mesh strainer set over a small bowl and use a rubber spatula to press out as much juice as possible. Discard the solids.

2. In a small saucepan set over medium heat, combine the granulated sugar, ⅓ cup (80 ml) water, and the reserved strawberry liquid. Cook for about 5 minutes, or until the sugar has dissolved and the syrup has thickened. Transfer to a bowl and allow to cool until ready to use.

FOR THE STRAWBERRY PASTRY CREAM

2 cups (480 ml) heavy cream

⅓ cup (68 g) plus ¼ cup (50 g) granulated sugar

⅛ teaspoon (0.5 g) fine sea salt

5 large egg yolks

½ cup (64 g) cornstarch

⅓ cup (107 g) seedless strawberry jam

¼ cup (½ stick/56 g) unsalted butter

2 teaspoons (10 ml) pure vanilla extract

FOR THE STRAWBERRY SYRUP

2 ounces (56 g or a heaping ⅓ cup) strawberries, fresh or frozen

3 tablespoons (38 g) granulated sugar

FOR THE CAKE

1¼ cups (2½ sticks/281 g) unsalted butter, room temperature, plus additional for greasing

3½ cups (439 g) all-purpose flour, plus additional for dusting

1½ cups (300 g) granulated sugar

6 large egg whites, room temperature

2 teaspoons (10 ml) almond extract

1 teaspoon (5 ml) pure vanilla extract

4 teaspoons (16 g) baking powder

½ teaspoon (2.5 g) fine sea salt

1½ cups (360 ml) whole milk

CONTINUED FROM PAGE 75

MAKE THE CAKE

1. Preheat the oven to 350°F (175°C). Grease and line three 6-inch (15-cm) round cake pans with parchment paper. Grease and flour the parchment paper. Set aside.

2. In the bowl of a stand mixer fitted with the paddle attachment, beat the butter and granulated sugar together on medium-high until pale and fluffy, about 4 minutes. With the mixer on low, add the egg whites, one at a time, and mix well after each addition. Add the almond and vanilla extracts and mix well.

3. In a medium bowl, whisk together the flour, baking powder, and salt. With the mixer set to low, add the flour mixture in three additions, alternating with the milk and scraping down the sides of the bowl with a rubber spatula as needed.

4. Divide the batter evenly among the prepared pans and bake for 30 to 40 minutes, or until a cake tester inserted into the centers comes out clean and the cakes are golden brown. Transfer the cakes to a wire rack to cool for 10 minutes before removing from the pans to cool completely.

MAKE THE MASCARPONE WHIPPED CREAM FROSTING

In the bowl of a stand mixer fitted with the whisk attachment, beat the heavy cream and powdered sugar on high until stiff peaks form. Add the mascarpone cheese and beat until the mascarpone is fully incorporated and the mixture is smooth. Refrigerate until ready to use.

ASSEMBLY

1. Using a serrated knife, level the cakes by trimming off the tops. Spread a small spoonful of frosting onto the center of a cake plate or stand to secure the cake, and place the first cake layer directly on top. Lightly brush the top of the cake with the strawberry syrup. Transfer about a third of the frosting to a piping bag fitted with a medium round pastry tip and pipe a ring of frosting around the top outer edge of the cake. Fill the center with about 3 tablespoons (45 ml) of strawberry pastry cream. Place the second cake layer on top and repeat the process (refrigerate any remaining pastry cream and syrup and reserve for another use).

2. Place the last cake layer on top and spread a thin layer of frosting around the sides and top of the cake using an offset palette knife. Transfer the cake to the refrigerator to allow the crumb coat to set, about 20 minutes.

3. Cover the sides and top of the cake with the remaining frosting. Using the tip of your palette knife, draw vertical lines up the sides of your cake and top with fresh strawberries.

Note: Preparing the strawberry syrup and strawberry pastry cream the night before will save you time on the day you plan to make this cake. Keep refrigerated until ready to serve.

FOR THE MASCARPONE WHIPPED CREAM FROSTING

1¼ cups (300 ml) heavy cream, cold

½ cup (60 g) powdered sugar

8 ounces (225 g) mascarpone cheese

FOR THE ASSEMBLY

2 cups (10 ounces/280 g) strawberries, for decoration

fallen apricot pistachio cake

I like to call this type of cake a "fallen cake" as it makes me think of fruit that's freshly tumbled off its tree—in this case, ripe summer apricots that were lucky enough to dive headfirst into sweet pistachio cake! The baked apricots keep this cake extremely moist, while the garnish of pistachios on top adds a nice layer of crunchy texture. SERVES 8

1. Preheat the oven to 300°F (150°C).

2. Line a baking tray with parchment paper, spread the ground pistachios on top, and roast for about 5 minutes, or until fragrant. Transfer to a wire rack to cool.

3. Turn the oven up to 350°F (175°C). Grease and line an 8-inch (20-cm) round springform pan with parchment paper. Grease and flour the parchment paper. Set aside.

4. In a medium bowl, whisk together the cooled ground pistachios, flour, baking powder, and salt.

5. In the bowl of a stand mixer fitted with the paddle attachment, beat the butter and granulated sugar together on medium-high until pale and fluffy, about 4 minutes. With the mixer on low, add the eggs, one at a time, and mix well after each addition. Add the buttermilk and mix until combined, then add the pistachio-flour mixture and mix until just combined.

6. Pour the batter into the prepared pan and arrange the apricots, cut side up, in a circular pattern. Bake for 35 to 40 minutes, or until a cake tester inserted into the center comes out clean and the cake is golden brown. Transfer the cake to a wire rack to cool for 15 minutes before unclasping the sides of the pan and gently lifting the cake off the bottom of the pan—grip the edge of parchment paper to gently slide it off the pan. Return the cake to the wire rack to cool completely.

7. Serve dusted with powdered sugar and decorated with chopped pistachios.

¾ cup (75 g) ground pistachios

11 tablespoons (155 g) unsalted butter, room temperature, plus additional for greasing

1 cup (125 g) all-purpose flour, plus additional for dusting

1 tablespoon (12 g) baking powder

½ teaspoon (2.5 g) fine sea salt

½ cup plus 2 tablespoons (125 g) granulated sugar

3 large eggs, room temperature

3 tablespoons (45 ml) buttermilk

18 ounces (510 g) apricots (about 10 apricots), pitted and cut in half

Powdered sugar, for dusting

¼ cup (40 g) chopped pistachios, for decorating

blooms in my basket: l'été

Like the season's hot and sultry days, flowers in the market feel a little wilder come summertime.
These are the bunches you'll see me happily carting home to fill up every vase in the place.

PEONIES. There's simply nothing more magical than witnessing the tight, round buds of pivoines open into lavishly full blooms. To me, these gloriously scented beauties are the standout of the season, and I'm always delighted to see them stacked in the stalls.

LISIANTHUS. Sweet and pretty lisianthus may look delicate, but they actually create strong, long-lasting bouquets. Often mistaken for roses, peonies, or poppies, they're full of grace and charisma and come in colors like apricot, ivory, mauve, and lilac.

ROSES. When in doubt, go classic. These timeless symbols of summer love are versatile enough to be enormous one-color bouquets or flirtatious nosegays in a petite pitcher from an antique market or weekend brocante. I've even been known to use their organic petals as decor for some of my cakes (see page 82).

DELPHINIUM. Tall, flowering stalks of delphinium or les pieds d'alouette are some of the season's most spectacular picks. Their summer spectrum—in blues, purples, whites, and soft pinks— make alluring displays in the salon of our apartment.

LAVENDER. The beloved rows of brilliant purple that pop up in Provence come June make for an easy excuse to travel down south. But lavender still makes its way into Paris's summertime markets, where you can buy it fresh for at-home arrangements, dried to use in scented sachets, or infused into items like honey and soap.

raspberry lemon rose tea cake

One of my earliest and fondest French pastry memories comes from a sliver of a shop on rue Bonaparte, home to the most exquisite confections in the city, crafted by the "Picasso of Pastry," Pierre Hermé. Before moving to Paris from California, we'd often visit family who lived on the Rive Gauche. I'd always make sure to stop by Hermé's temple of patisserie perfection, where I'd scan rows of glittering macarons and immaculate pastries whose names I couldn't pronounce in search of one thing: the croissant Ispahan, the chef's signature that had a tendency to sell out early. Featuring a flavor I find absolutely irresistible, the famous croissant is composed of raspberries, rose cream, rose petals, and lychees. Hermé adapted his Ispahan croissant, which he drizzles with a heady rosewater glaze, into macarons and cakes. I distinctly remember strolling from the shop to the nearby Luxembourg Gardens, where I'd daydream of what it might be like to indulge in one every day if I lived in the city. Now that I actually call Paris home, I reserve the croissant for special occasions—but it still provides endless inspiration for my baking. This tea cake finds its muse in those flavors, but with my own twist: I omit the lychee in favor of lemon. SERVES 8

MAKE THE TEA CAKE

1. Preheat the oven to 325°F (165°C). Grease and line an 8-x-4-inch (20-x-10-cm) loaf pan with parchment paper, covering the bottom and long sides of the pan and leaving a 1-inch (2.5-cm) overhang on both long sides. Set aside.

2. In a small bowl, rub the lemon zest into the granulated sugar with your fingers. Transfer to the bowl of a stand mixer fitted with the paddle attachment, add the butter, and beat on medium until light and fluffy, about 4 minutes. Add the eggs, one at a time, scraping down the sides of the bowl between additions. Add the lemon juice and vanilla and beat until incorporated.

3. In a medium bowl, whisk together the flour, baking soda, baking powder, and salt. With the mixer on low, add the flour mixture in three additions, alternating with the buttermilk. Gently fold in the raspberries using a rubber spatula—it's okay if some of the raspberries tear, as it will add color to your batter.

FOR THE TEA CAKE

8 tablespoons (1 stick/113 g) unsalted butter, room temperature, plus additional for greasing

2 tablespoons (12 g) grated lemon zest (from 2 lemons)

1 cup (200 g) granulated sugar

3 large eggs, room temperature

2 tablespoons (30 ml) freshly squeezed lemon juice (from 1 lemon)

1 teaspoon (5 ml) pure vanilla extract

1½ cups (189 g) all-purpose flour

¼ teaspoon (1 g) baking soda

¼ teaspoon (1 g) baking powder

¼ teaspoon (1 g) fine sea salt

½ cup (120 ml) buttermilk

1 cup (4⅓ ounces/126 g) raspberries

FOR THE RASPBERRY ROSE GLAZE

½-¾ cups (7-8 ounces/187-219 g) fresh raspberries, plus additional for decorating

1 cup (125 g) powdered sugar

1 teaspoon (5 ml) rose water

1 tablespoon (15 ml) whole milk or heavy cream, plus additional as needed

Sugared organic rose petals, for decorating (optional, see page 84)

4. Pour the batter into the prepared pan and bake 55 to 60 minutes, or until a cake tester comes out clean and the cake is golden brown. Transfer the cake to a wire rack to cool for 15 minutes before using the parchment paper overhang to lift the cake out of the pan. Return the cake to the wire rack to cool completely.

MAKE THE RASPBERRY ROSE GLAZE

1. Meanwhile, in a small saucepan, heat the raspberries over medium-low heat for 5 to 6 minutes to release their juices. Pour through a fine-mesh strainer set over a small bowl and use a rubber spatula to press out as much juice as possible. Discard the solids. Return the strained raspberry juice to the pan and cook over medium heat until reduced to about $\frac{1}{4}$ cup (60 ml); set aside to cool.

2. Once the raspberry juice is cool, add the powdered sugar and rose water and whisk to combine. Gradually add the milk or heavy cream, whisking until well combined and smooth. Add more milk or cream as needed to create a thick but pourable glaze.

3. Place a sheet of parchment paper underneath the rack holding the cooled cake. Starting at one end, pour the glaze over the cake, letting it drip down the sides and going back and forth from one end to the other to completely cover the cake. Decorate with fresh raspberries and sugared organic rose petals, if using (see Cake Decor That Sparkles, page 84). Allow the glaze to set at room temperature for about 15 minutes before serving.

cake decor that sparkles

Give your baking some sparkling personality with easy decorative sugared flower petals and leaves, fruit (think cranberries or blueberries), and herbs, such as sprigs of rosemary. While not edible, these sugared items lend a definite flair to baked goods. In addition to whatever items you'd like to sugar, you need only two ingredients: 1 large egg white, and superfine or granulated sugar (up to 1 cup/200 g, depending on how many items you wish to sugar). Sugared flowers can be stored in an airtight container at room temperature for up to three days.

Here's how to do it:

1) In a bowl, beat the egg white until frothy.

2) Using a pastry brush, lightly paint an even layer of the egg white onto an item you wish to sugar.

3) Coat the item with superfine sugar by carefully rolling it in a bowl of the sugar or by spooning the sugar over it. Gently tap off any excess.

4) Place on a baking sheet lined with parchment or wax paper and allow to completely dry, 2 to 3 hours.

5) Decorate your cake as desired.

chocolate cherry layer cake

The combination of flavors in this cake—chocolate, cherry, and vanilla—makes me recall that quintessential American summertime dessert, the ice cream sundae. Growing up, I never missed a chance to indulge in one at Farrell's Ice Cream Parlour, a local San Diego restaurant famous for its endless ice cream sundae iterations that sadly closed its doors in 2019. I simply had to channel this summertime childhood favorite into cake form: a chocolate layer cake filled with cherries and covered in vanilla buttercream. Feel free to serve with a generous scoop or two of vanilla ice cream! SERVES 12

MAKE THE CHOCOLATE CAKE

1. Preheat the oven to 350°F (175°C). Grease and line three 6-inch (15-cm) round cake pans with parchment paper. Grease the parchment paper and dust the pans with cocoa powder. Set aside.

2. In a large bowl, whisk together the flour, granulated sugar, sifted cocoa powder, baking powder, baking soda, and salt. In a slow steady stream, pour the hot coffee into the flour mixture while mixing. Add the buttermilk and whisk until incorporated. Add the oil and whisk until incorporated. Add the eggs, one at a time, mixing well after each addition. Add the vanilla and give the batter one last stir.

3. Divide the batter evenly among the prepared pans and bake for 30 to 35 minutes, or until a cake tester inserted into the centers comes out clean—the cakes will crack on top and have a slightly crunchy crust. Transfer the cakes to a wire rack to cool for 15 minutes before removing from the pans to cool completely.

MAKE THE ITALIAN MERINGUE BUTTERCREAM

1. In a small saucepan set over high heat, combine the granulated sugar and ¼ cup (60 ml) water. Bring to a boil and continue cooking until the syrup reaches soft-ball stage, or 240°F (115°C) on a candy thermometer, 8 to 10 minutes.

2. Meanwhile, in the bowl of a stand mixer fitted with the whisk attachment, whisk the egg whites and salt on high until stiff peaks form.

3. Once the syrup has reached 240°F (115°C), carefully pour it into the egg white mixture in a slow steady stream with the mixer on low. Once all the syrup has been added, turn the mixer up to high and whisk until cool, about 5 minutes.

FOR THE CHOCOLATE CAKE

Unsalted butter, for greasing

½ cup (50 g) Dutch-process cocoa powder, sifted, plus additional for dusting

2½ cups (315 g) all-purpose flour

2 cups (400 g) granulated sugar

2 teaspoons (8 g) baking powder

2 teaspoons (8 g) baking soda

½ teaspoon (2.5 g) fine sea salt

1 cup (240 ml) strongly brewed coffee, hot

1 cup (240 ml) buttermilk

½ cup (120 ml) sunflower oil

2 large eggs, room temperature

1½ teaspoons (7.5 ml) pure vanilla extract

FOR THE ITALIAN MERINGUE BUTTERCREAM

1 cup (200 g) granulated sugar

4 large egg whites

⅛ teaspoon (.5 g) fine sea salt

2 cups (4 sticks/450 g) unsalted butter, room temperature

2 teaspoons (10 ml) pure vanilla extract

CONTINUED FROM PAGE 87

4. With the mixer set to medium-high, add the butter, 1 tablespoon (14 g) at a time, until fully combined. Once all the butter has been added, add the vanilla and whip on high until light and fluffy, 4 to 5 minutes more.

MAKE THE CHERRY FILLING

In a medium saucepan set over low heat, combine the cherries, granulated sugar, lemon juice, and ¼ cup (60 ml) water. Bring to a simmer, stirring occasionally, until the sugar dissolves. Add the cornstarch and cook on low heat, stirring, until the mixture thickens, 5 to 6 minutes. Transfer to a glass jar and allow to cool completely before using.

ASSEMBLY

1. Using a serrated knife, level the cakes by trimming off the tops. Spread a small spoonful of buttercream in the center of a cake plate or stand to secure the cake, and place the first cake layer directly on top. Transfer about a third of the buttercream to a piping bag fitted with a medium round pastry tip and pipe a circle around the top outer edge of the cake. Fill the circle with about ¼ cup (60 ml) of the cherry filling. Place the next cake layer on top and repeat the process.

2. Place the last layer on top and spread a thin layer of buttercream over the top and sides of the cake using an offset palette knife. Transfer the cake to the refrigerator to allow the crumb coat to set, about 20 minutes.

3. Spread the remaining buttercream over the sides and top of the cake. Decorate the top with cherries. Use a vegetable peeler to shave some of the dark chocolate bar then gently press the chocolate shavings around the bottom of the cake.

Notes: Leftover cherry filling makes a delightful topping for ice cream or your morning yogurt. I also love it served alongside a pile of crunchy meringue.

FOR THE CHERRY FILLING

2 cups (7 ounces/200 g) cherries, pitted

¼ cup (50 g) granulated sugar

1 tablespoon (15 ml) freshly squeezed lemon juice (from 1 lemon)

1 tablespoon (8 g) cornstarch

FOR THE ASSEMBLY

12 cherries

2 ounces (56 g) 70% dark chocolate, for shaving

white peach tart

When stone fruit season is in full swing, I often mull over whether to buy yellow or white peaches while in line at the marché. Inevitably I'll ask for the vendor's advice on what's best at the moment . . . and that, in turn, leads to a typical market chat about what I intend to do with said peaches. "Are they to eat now or to bake with later, monsieur?" I'll be asked. And when I tell them it's for a tart, I'll often hear, "Choose white." Pêches blanches are celebrated for their delicate and richly perfumed floral notes and are also slightly sweeter than their yellow counterparts, making them ideal in tarts. When baked together with almond frangipane, the aroma is absolutely intoxicating. I like to serve a slice with a big dollop of crème fraîche. SERVES 8 TO 10

FOR THE ALMOND TART DOUGH

1⅔ cups (210 g) all-purpose flour

⅔ cup (84 g) powdered sugar

¼ cup (28 g) almond flour

8 tablespoons (1 stick/113 g) unsalted butter, room temperature

2 large egg yolks, lightly beaten

Pinch of fine sea salt

FOR THE FRANGIPANE FILLING

¾ cup (150 g) granulated sugar

8 tablespoons (1 stick/113 g) unsalted butter, room temperature

2 large eggs, room temperature

1 cup (112 g) almond flour

1 teaspoon (5 ml) almond extract

1 tablespoon (8 g) all-purpose flour

FOR THE ASSEMBLY

5 white peaches

Crème fraîche or whipped cream, for serving

MAKE THE ALMOND TART DOUGH

1. In the bowl of a stand mixer fitted with the paddle attachment, combine the flour, powdered sugar, almond flour, butter, egg yolks, and salt on low until a dough forms. Do not overmix. When the dough comes together, shape into a disc and wrap in plastic wrap. Refrigerate the dough until firm, at least 1 hour.

2. Remove the almond tart dough from the refrigerator 30 minutes before you plan to roll it out. Preheat the oven to 400°F (200°C). Transfer the dough to a lightly floured work surface and roll out to a large circle, about 12 inches (30 cm) in diameter. Carefully roll the dough around the rolling pin, brushing off any excess flour. Unroll the dough over a 9-inch (23-cm) tart pan with a removable bottom, gently tuck it into the pan, and trim any excess dough. Using a fork, poke tiny holes across the bottom of the tart shell. Line the tart shell with parchment paper and fill with pie weights to keep the dough from puffing up during baking. Bake for 10 minutes. Remove the tart shell from the oven and carefully remove the pie weights and parchment paper. Return the tart shell to the oven and bake for an additional 10 to 12 minutes, or until the center turns golden. Transfer the tart shell to a wire rack to cool completely.

MAKE THE FRANGIPANE FILLING

Meanwhile, in a medium bowl, whisk together the granulated sugar and butter by hand until pale, about 4 minutes. Beat in the eggs until combined, then add the almond flour and almond extract and whisk until smooth. Add the flour and whisk once more until fully incorporated. Refrigerate until ready to use.

CONTINUED FROM PAGE 89

ASSEMBLY

1. Spread the frangipane filling evenly in the cooled tart shell.

2. Cut the peaches in half and discard the pits. Cut each peach lengthwise into thin slices—cut all the way through the peaches but keep the slices together so they still form a half.

3. Arrange the peach halves snugly in the frangipane and slightly fan out the slices. Bake for 30 to 35 minutes, or until the pastry is golden brown. Serve with crème fraîche or a dollop of whipped cream.

lavender honey madeleines

Much has been written about the madeleine—that perfect little shell-shaped sponge cake noted for its buttery simplicity. Its size is ideal to hide away in pockets for a petite treat on the go or to pack in picnic baskets for sharing with a friend Seine-side.

If you've ever visited the region of Provence in June or July, then you probably know the air is sweetened with the scent of endless fields of lavender. I first tasted lavender honey in Saint-Saturnin-les-Apt, a village perched high in the Luberon region surrounded by large swathes of vibrant violet. I found it remarkable for its light fragrance and immediately thought about using the honey as a sweetener in my next batch of madeleines. Much like Marcel Proust's own tea-dipped madeleine rapture, when the aroma of lavender baking in these mini cakes fills my kitchen, I'm transported right back to those tiny towns nestled so perfectly into picturesque fields of Provençal purple. Depending on how many molds your madeleine pan has (most pans have 12 molds), you will need to make 2-3 batches with this recipe. MAKES 30 MADELEINES

13 tablespoons (182 g) unsalted butter, melted and cooled to room temperature, plus additional for greasing

1¼ cups plus 3 tablespoons (181 g) all-purpose flour, plus additional for dusting

1¼ teaspoons (5 g) baking powder

¼ teaspoon (1 g) fine sea salt

4 large eggs

½ cup (120 ml) lavender honey (or any single-varietal wildflower honey)

Powdered sugar, for dusting

1. Grease and flour a madeleine pan. Place in the freezer to chill for 30 minutes. Preheat the oven to 400°F (200°C).

2. In a small bowl, whisk together the flour, baking powder, and salt; set aside.

3. In the bowl of a stand mixer fitted with the whisk attachment, combine the eggs and honey and whip for about 10 minutes, or until thick pale ribbons start to appear in the batter. Add the flour mixture and use a rubber spatula to fold until just combined. Add the melted butter and fold until just combined. Fill each madeleine mold with about 1 tablespoon (15 ml) of batter. Bake for about 6 minutes, or until the madeleines are golden brown. Remove from the pan and let cool completely on a wire rack.

4. Serve dusted with powdered sugar or dipped into your next cup of coffee.

pavlova with summer berries

The pavlova is an internationally irresistible summertime dessert boasting a delicately crisp outer shell of meringue that hides a chewy marshmallowy center, which is then topped with freshly whipped cream and summer fruits. Heating the sugar before adding it to the whipped egg whites results in a meringue with a beautiful glossy sheen. I like to use different strawberry varieties for texture and a smattering of darker berries for contrast. It's a meringue cloud of perfection that is best shared, so grab a spoon and dig in family style! I like to prepare the meringue the night before, so it has time to dry out in the oven and is ready to be filled come dessert. SERVES 6 TO 8

FOR THE MERINGUE

1½ cups (300 g) superfine sugar

5½ ounces (154 g) egg whites (approximately 4 large egg whites)

Pinch of fine sea salt

1 teaspoon (5 ml) pure vanilla extract

Note: This type of meringue needs to be measured precisely, so it's best to weigh the superfine sugar and egg whites.

FOR THE WHIPPED CREAM

1 cup (240 ml) heavy cream, cold

2 tablespoons (15 g) powdered sugar

½ teaspoon (2.5 ml) pure vanilla extract

FOR THE ASSEMBLY

2 cups (10 ounces/280 g) mixed summer berries, such as raspberries, blackberries, strawberries, and red currants

MAKE THE MERINGUE

1. Preheat the oven to 400°F (200°C). Line a baking tray with parchment paper, spread the superfine sugar on top, and bake for 7 minutes.

2. Meanwhile, in the bowl of a stand mixer fitted with the whisk attachment, combine the egg whites and salt. With the mixer on low, whisk slowly at first, allowing small stabilizing bubbles to form, then gradually increase the speed to medium and then high and whip until stiff peaks start to form.

3. Take the sugar out of the oven and turn the temperature down to 225°F (105°C). With the mixer on high, gradually add the hot sugar, 1 tablespoon (12.5 g) at a time. Add the vanilla and continue mixing on high until the meringue has a smooth, glossy texture, 5 to 6 minutes.

4. Line a baking tray with a fresh sheet of parchment paper. Spoon the meringue onto the center of the tray and use an offset palette knife to shape it into a large, domed mound. Use the palette knife to make a roughly 1-inch (2.5-cm) deep indentation in the middle of the meringue, creating a nest that will eventually hold whipped cream and fruit. Bake for 40 to 45 minutes, or until the parchment paper easily peels off the meringue. Turn off the oven and leave the meringue to dry out in the oven for several hours or overnight.

MAKE THE WHIPPED CREAM

In the bowl of a stand mixer fitted with the whisk attachment, beat the heavy cream, powdered sugar, and vanilla together on high until stiff peaks form, 3 to 4 minutes.

ASSEMBLY

When ready to serve, dollop the whipped cream into the center of the meringue nest and top with mixed summer berries.

vanilla bean panna cotta

If summertime really is when the livin' is easy, as Ella Fitzgerald so beautifully croons, then panna cotta is perfectly matched to the season. It's always an elegant and refreshing choice for a warm summer evening soirée. Sweetened vanilla bean cream provides a heavenly base for a tart rhubarb sauce. I like to serve these in various-sized glasses alongside a plate of buttery sablés called punitions that I often stock up on from Poilâne Bakery on rue Debelleyme in the Marais. SERVES 4

MAKE THE RHUBARB SAUCE

In a large saucepan set over low heat, combine the rhubarb, granulated sugar, orange juice, and ¼ cup (60 ml) water and bring to a simmer. Continue simmering until the rhubarb is tender and the syrup is thick, 8 to 10 minutes. Transfer to a shallow dish to cool.

MAKE THE PANNA COTTA

1. In a small bowl, sprinkle the gelatin over the boiling water, stir, and allow to bloom, 3 to 5 minutes.

2. In a small saucepan set over medium heat, combine the heavy cream and granulated sugar. Using the tip of a sharp knife, scrape the seeds from the vanilla bean into the pan and bring to a gentle boil, stirring occasionally. Add the bloomed gelatin mixture and stir until incorporated. Turn off the heat.

3. Divide the mixture among four glasses or ramekins and allow to cool to room temperature. Transfer to the refrigerator to set, at least 3 hours or overnight.

4. Add 2 or 3 pieces of rhubarb, along with some rhubarb syrup, to each glass before serving.

Note: You'll have a fair bit of extra rhubarb sauce left from this recipe. It makes an excellent topping over ice cream or your morning yogurt!

FOR THE RHUBARB SAUCE

1 pound (450 g/4 to 5 large stalks or 7 to 8 small stalks) rhubarb, cut into 1½-inch (3.5-cm) batons

½ cup plus 2 tablespoons (125 g) granulated sugar

2 tablespoons (30 ml) freshly squeezed orange juice

FOR THE PANNA COTTA

2½ teaspoons (7.5 g) powdered gelatin

1 tablespoon (15 ml) boiling water

2 cups plus 4 teaspoons (500 ml) heavy cream

¼ cup (50 g) granulated sugar

1 vanilla bean, split lengthwise
(see page 73 for vanilla bean note)

passionfruit coconut cake

I love this tangy passionfruit curd so much that I decided to have it as the starring flavor in the cake for our fête de fiançailles (engagement party) at the beautiful Château de Bosgouet in Normandy. One of my dearest friends, Jennifer Drew, who also happens to be a talented baker, flew in from Australia for the occasion—and to help me with the cake! The summer garden party–themed affair was meant to take place outdoors among the two-hundred-year-old linden trees that fill the groves facing the Napoleonic château. Sadly, however, the region's famously unpredictable weather had other plans. Once all our guests had been led out into the garden for champagne and nibbles, dark clouds suddenly rolled in, forcing us to make a mad dash through the rain and back indoors. We, of course, had a fabulous party nonetheless, and I'll always remember bringing this cake out to the delighted candlelit faces of some of our closest friends. Jen and I made sure to keep a jar of the passionfruit curd handy, as we both knew there would be requests for an extra dollop on the side, so feel free to do the same. SERVES 10 TO 12

MAKE THE COCONUT CAKE

1. Preheat the oven to 350°F (175°C). Grease and line three 8-inch (20-cm) round cake pans with parchment paper. Grease and flour the parchment paper. Set aside.

2. In a medium bowl, whisk together the eggs, egg whites, milk, coconut cream, and vanilla; set aside.

3. In the bowl of a stand mixer fitted with the paddle attachment, combine the flour, granulated sugar, baking powder, and salt. Mix on low until combined. With the mixer on low, add the softened butter, 1 tablespoon (14 g) at a time, and mix well after each addition. Once all the butter has been added, slowly add half of the milk mixture and mix on medium-high until smooth. With the mixer turned back to low, add the remaining milk mixture and mix until just combined. Using a rubber spatula, give the batter one final mix.

4. Divide the batter evenly among the prepared pans and bake for 35 to 40 minutes, or until a cake tester inserted into the centers comes out clean and the cakes are golden brown. Transfer the cakes to a wire rack to cool 10 minutes before removing from the pans to cool completely.

FOR THE COCONUT CAKE

1½ cups (3 sticks/336 g) unsalted butter, room temperature, plus additional for greasing

4¾ cups (594 g) all-purpose flour, plus additional for dusting

2 large eggs, room temperature

4 large egg whites, room temperature

1½ cups plus 1 tablespoon (375 ml) whole milk

¾ cup (180 ml) coconut cream (see page 50)

1 teaspoon (5 ml) pure vanilla extract

2 cups (400 g) granulated sugar

1 tablespoon (12 g) baking powder

½ teaspoon (2.5 g) fine sea salt

FOR THE PASSIONFRUIT CURD

11 passionfruit

2 large eggs

2 large egg yolks

¾ cup (150 g) granulated sugar

¾ cup (1½ sticks/170 g) unsalted butter

1 tablespoon (15 ml) freshly squeezed lemon juice

CONTINUED FROM PAGE 98

MAKE THE PASSIONFRUIT CURD

1. Meanwhile, cut 1 passionfruit in half, scoop out the flesh and seeds, and set aside. Discard the skin. Cut the remaining 10 passionfruit in half, scoop out the flesh, and place the flesh in a food processor to separate from the seeds. Pulse the fruit until smooth, then pour through a fine-mesh strainer set over a bowl and use a rubber spatula to press out as much juice as possible; set aside. Discard the solids.

2. In a small bowl, whisk together the eggs, egg yolks, and granulated sugar until smooth, about 4 minutes.

3. In a medium saucepan set over low heat, melt the butter, then add the egg mixture, the strained passionfruit, and lemon juice. Cook, whisking continuously, until the curd thickens, about 6 minutes. Remove from the heat, add the reserved passionfruit flesh and seeds, and gently stir to incorporate. Transfer to a glass bowl and cover with plastic wrap, pressing it directly onto the surface of the curd to prevent a skin forming. Refrigerate until cold.

MAKE THE ITALIAN MERINGUE BUTTERCREAM

1. Combine the granulated sugar and ¼ cup (60 ml) water in a small saucepan set over high heat. Bring to a boil and continue cooking until the syrup reaches soft-ball stage, or 240°F (115°C) on a candy thermometer, 8 to 10 minutes.

2. Meanwhile, in the bowl of a stand mixer fitted with the whisk attachment, whisk the egg whites and salt on high until stiff peaks form.

3. Once the syrup has reached 240°F (115°C), pour it into the egg white mixture in a slow steady stream with the mixer on low. Once all the syrup has been added, turn the mixer up to high and whisk until cool, about 5 minutes. With the mixer set to medium-high, add the butter, 1 tablespoon (14 g) at a time, until fully combined. Once all the butter has been added, add the vanilla and beat on high until light and fluffy, 4 to 5 minutes more.

ASSEMBLY

1. Using a serrated knife, level the cakes by trimming off the tops. Spread a small spoonful of buttercream onto the center of a cake plate or stand to secure the cake, and place the first cake layer directly on top.

2. Divide the buttercream into thirds and set aside a third for covering the cake and a third to decorate the cake.

FOR THE ITALIAN MERINGUE BUTTERCREAM

1 cup (200 g) granulated sugar

4 large egg whites

⅛ teaspoon (0.5 g) fine sea salt

2 cups (4 sticks/450 g) unsalted butter, room temperature

2 teaspoons (10 ml) pure vanilla extract

Yellow food coloring gel, such as Wilton (optional)

3. Transfer most of the remaining buttercream to a piping bag fitted with a medium round pastry tip. Pipe a circle around the top outer edge of the cake, then fill the circle with about ¼ cup (60 ml) of the passionfruit curd, spreading it to evenly fill the circle. Place the next cake layer on top and repeat the process. Place the last cake layer on top.

4. Using the rest of that portion of buttercream, spread a thin layer of buttercream around the sides and top of the cake using an offset palette knife. Transfer the cake to the refrigerator to allow the crumb coat to set, about 20 minutes.

5. Spread another third of the buttercream on the sides and top of the cake to cover.

6. If coloring the buttercream for decorating, gradually add color to the remaining third of buttercream by dipping just the tip of a wooden toothpick into the food coloring gel and then swirling the color into the buttercream. Mix the buttercream to incorporate the color, gradually adding more food coloring gel until you get the shade you like. Transfer the colored buttercream to a piping bag fitted with a medium French star pastry tip and pipe dollops of buttercream in a ring around the top of the finished cake.

must-not-miss summer experiences in paris

1) Take to the Seine and enjoy a night cruise on a Bateaux-Mouches river boat and watch as the City of Light comes alive in all its sparkly splendor.

2) Revel in the streets during Fête de la Musique in June, the much-anticipated music celebration when Parisians meet up outdoors to catch the various concerts playing all night long in the public spaces and parks of each arrondissement.

3) Celebrate La Fête Nationale, or Bastille Day, on July 14 with a bottle of champagne on the Champ-de-Mars to catch the stellar fireworks display at the Eiffel Tower. (Want to skip the crowds? Watch from a bridge or find a hotel—or a friend—with a terrace view!)

4) Rent a bike or grab a Vélib'— a bike from the city's bicycle-sharing system—and venture on one of Paris's many bicycle paths. My favorite time to do this is in August, when the city empties out and becomes village-like, free from the usual hustle and bustle.

5) Journey just forty-five minutes outside Paris and be dazzled by Les Soirées aux Chandelles at the Château de Vaux-le-Vicomte, when more than two thousand candles illuminate the grounds and formal gardens of the historic château every Saturday evening.

chapter 3

l'automne

{ fall }

WITH APOLOGIES TO perky Doris Day films and tunes crooned by Ella Fitzgerald, my personal "Paris in the spring" moment is . . . Paris in the fall. Contrary to popular belief, autumn is the season La Ville Lumière experiences its true reawakening, and much of it is due to the magic that is la rentrée or "the return." Technically, it's the start of the new school year. But in reality, it's a rebirth, a period when Parisians begin pouring back into the city post-vacances. August's sleepy days are officially done, and what was once an empty summertime ghost town suddenly fills to the brim. Streets are jam-packed, you're elbow to elbow on the metro, and stores and restaurants have flung back open their doors. The buzzy energy of a city hitting restart is palpable.

Truth be told, this is the time when Paris puts on its finest show. And all it asks of you is to sit back and watch.

It starts first in the capital's ubiquitous cafés, their terraces now overflowing onto the sidewalks with patrons reconnecting after a month away, or sipping a drink, or simply smoking another cigarette. If you look closely, you'll notice their woven rattan chairs turned not inward toward the table, but out, facing the street. That's because cafés are a prime location for one of autumn's most anticipated activities: people watching. Thanks to pitch-perfect weather—not too hot, not yet too cold—the beloved Parisian pastime goes full throttle in the fall, when the parade of passersby is best enjoyed over a coffee, a hot pot of tea, or, if you're in Saint-Germain-des-Prés at Café de Flore, with a cup of hot chocolate warming your hands.

The gawking only gets better come the end of September, during Paris Fashion Week. When legendary brands the likes of Dior, Chanel, and Saint Laurent stage their runways within some of the city's most glamorous venues, the spirit of stylishness spills out onto the avenues.

But the show doesn't stop there.

It continues into Parisian parks, where you can pull up an iconic green armchair, a newspaper in hand, and watch the world promenade past. An added benefit? The foliage that's rustling overhead, boasting its own fashionable fall palette of crimson, blazing orange, and gold. As a former desert dweller whose hometown greenery consisted of only green palm trees and cacti, I admit that the changing of leaves is something that continues to captivate me. I remember our first autumn in Paris, being wowed while in the Tuileries and the Parc des Buttes-Chaumont as we crunched through the leaves and watched our dog Parker jump headfirst into big, irresistible piles of the stuff. Autumn-color hunting is now our annual tradition, with the initial stops being the rows of box trees at my favorite parc palais, Jardin du Palais-Royal, and in our neighborhood's own place des Vosges, where the benches make the perfect spot to take in the showcase (and enjoy an afternoon goûter with a chocolate financier). And when we're ready to see something extraordinarily vibrant, we'll take a short train ride to Parc de Sceaux or Fontainebleau, dog in arms and basket in hand, where we'll picnic with an Apple Cardamom Tea Cake (page 126) under a canopy of wild fall color.

It never disappoints. And neither does what shows up at the autumn markets.

It should be no surprise that the spectacle makes its way into many a marché, like my closest market on Tuesday and Friday mornings, the Marché Popincourt, which begins to welcome the season's brightest star, the mirabelle plum, which I love to use in my Mirabelle Upside-Down

Cake (page 117) at the tail end of summer and on through September. Though the petite golden plum commands a lot of attention—often dominating tart trays at boulangeries and making cameos as the month's specialty jam at cafés—it still shares the stage with prunes, purply quetsch plums, which I love to roast and spoon over pound cake (see page 136); persimmons (or *kaki*, as they're called here), which bake up beautifully in a Bundt cake (see page 111); and figs you can drizzle with honey, pair with goat cheese, or simply eat raw. Raspberries, blackberries, and blueberries are all still available, usually through October. Just before mirabelles take their bow, sometime in the middle of September, the grape harvest arrives, along with winter squash, nuts, and mushrooms with the names girolles, cèpes, and trompettes de la mort handwritten on the signs announcing their debut. In adjacent flower stalls, an audience of burnt-orange dahlias gaze out, their giant heads lowered for a better look at the piles of apples, pears, and quince taking their turn in the spotlight, depending on the variety, throughout the season.

It's these fruits especially that motivate me to make my own return—this time to richer, heavier baking, especially after the summer and spring months, when we like to keep things light. This is the portion of the year when we transition, when we ease back into the things that comfort us and keep us cozy as the air turns crisp. For me, that means layering up in knotted scarves and woolen sweaters, hosting more friends and tea parties in our home, looking for new baking ideas both in the seasonal flavors I adore—like caramel, brown sugar, maple, cinnamon, and coffee— and the bounty of sights, smells, and tastes that an autumn in Paris offers me as inspiration.

And I, for one, am here for the show.

cinnamon swirl bundt cake

This cinnamon swirl Bundt cake has been near and dear to my heart since childhood, as it's always been my mother's signature cake. Her version incorporates sour cream, which I substitute here with crème fraîche, because it has a richer flavor due to its higher fat content. Everything else, however, I've kept the same, right down to the maple glaze she would allow me to pour—with a watchful eye. SERVES 12

MAKE THE CAKE

1. Preheat the oven to 350°F (175°C). Grease and flour a 10- to 12-cup (2.4- to 2.8-L) Bundt pan or use baking spray; set aside.

2. In a medium bowl, whisk together the flour, baking powder, and salt; set aside.

3. In the bowl of a stand mixer fitted with the paddle attachment, beat the butter and granulated sugar together until pale and fluffy, about 4 minutes. With the mixer on low, add the eggs, one at a time, scraping down the sides of the bowl with a rubber spatula between additions. Add the crème fraîche and vanilla and mix until just combined. With the mixer on low, add the flour mixture in three additions, mixing until just combined. Transfer about 2 cups (480 ml) to a medium bowl. Add the dark brown sugar, cinnamon, and milk, and stir until smooth. Pour about a third of the plain cake batter into the bottom of the prepared Bundt pan, then pour about half of the cinnamon batter on top. Repeat to add a second layer of plain batter, followed by a second layer of cinnamon batter. Finish with a third layer of plain batter on top. To make the marble swirl, use the point of a butter knife to draw a zigzag pattern through the batter. Bake for 55 to 60 minutes, or until a cake tester inserted into the center comes out clean and the cake is golden brown. Transfer the cake to a wire rack to cool for 15 minutes before carefully removing from the pan to cool completely.

MAKE THE MAPLE GLAZE

1. Meanwhile, in a small bowl, whisk together the powdered sugar, maple syrup, and vanilla until well combined and smooth. Add more powdered sugar or maple syrup as needed to create a thick but pourable glaze.

2. Place a sheet of parchment paper underneath the rack holding the cooled cake. Slowly pour the glaze over the top of the cake, allowing it to drip down the sides. Allow the glaze to set at room temperature for about 15 minutes before serving.

FOR THE CAKE

1 cup (2 sticks/225 g) unsalted butter, at room temperature, plus additional for greasing

3 cups (375 g) all-purpose flour, plus additional for dusting

2 teaspoons (8 g) baking powder

½ teaspoon (2.5 g) fine sea salt

2 cups (400 g) granulated sugar

5 large eggs

8 ounces (225 g) crème fraîche

1 tablespoon (15 ml) pure vanilla extract

¼ cup (55 g) firmly packed dark brown sugar

2 tablespoons (12 g) ground cinnamon

2 tablespoons (30 ml) whole milk

FOR THE MAPLE GLAZE

1 cup (125 g) powdered sugar, plus additional as needed

¼ cup (60 ml) real maple syrup, plus additional as needed

½ teaspoon (2.5 ml) pure vanilla extract

must-not-miss autumn experiences in paris

1) Get a unique (and free) peek inside many of Paris's monuments, institutes, museums, and historic buildings not normally accessible to the public as they temporarily open their doors in September's annual Heritage Days, Les Journées du Patrimoine. I recommend getting inside the halls of La Sorbonne and its glorious library, and the gilded rooms of the Élysée Palace are always a highlight.

2) On the first Saturday in October, head out for a festive art all-nighter with Nuit Blanche. From 7:00 pm to 7:00 am, you'll be inspired by original and avant-garde experiences by international artists installed all across the city. The Paris City Hall counts about twenty restaurants that stay open until very late throughout the city to feed hungry revelers.

3) Take a stroll through the beautiful gardens of Paris, namely the Jardin du Luxembourg and Jardin des Tuileries, which do the autumn season like no other. Be sure to bundle up in scarves and sweaters and bring a blanket for a picnic with a Tarte Normande (page 116)!

4) Go farther afield for a day in the orchards at Les Fermes de Gally, just next door to Versailles. You can spend an afternoon picking fall fruits—apples, pears, and quinces—then bring them back to bake up an Apple Cardamom Tea Cake (page 126) or a spicy pear galette (see page 118).

tarte normande

We love visiting Normandy for its famed cheeses (like creamy rounds of Camembert and heart-shaped Neufchâtel), charming thatched houses called chaumièrer, and, of course, endless slices of tarte Normande! This classic French tart is meant to be quite rustic in appearance, comprised of apples and cream infused with Calvados (apple brandy) baked inside a buttery pâte sablée base. The creamy egg custard gets nicely caramelized after baking, and I like to add a sprinkling of lightly toasted almond slices at the end. Don't fret if your crust is a little uneven as mine sometimes is; your guests will overlook anything that smells this good right out of the oven. SERVES 6

MAKE THE PÂTE SABLÉE

1. In a medium bowl, whisk together the flour, powdered sugar, and salt. Add the cubed butter and rub into the flour with your fingers until the mixture resembles coarse sand. Add the egg and use a fork to mix the dough until it just comes together and there are no dry bits left. Using your hands, form the dough into a ball and wrap in plastic wrap. Refrigerate the dough until firm, at least 1 hour.

2. Remove the pâte sablée from the refrigerator 30 minutes before you plan to roll it out. Grease and flour a 9-inch (23-cm) tart pan with a removable bottom. Transfer the dough to a lightly floured work surface and roll out to a large circle, about 12 inches (30 cm) in diameter. Carefully roll the dough around the rolling pin, brushing off any excess flour. Unroll the dough over the prepared pan, gently tuck it into the pan, and trim any excess dough. Return to the refrigerator to chill for 20 minutes.

MAKE THE APPLE FILLING

1. Meanwhile, preheat the oven to 350°F (175°C).

2. Peel the apples and slice them in half lengthwise; remove and discard the cores. Cut each apple half lengthwise into slices—cut all the way through the apples but keep the slices together so they still form a half. Arrange the apple halves (there should be 6 in total) in the chilled tart shell and fan the slices to create a flower.

3. In a small bowl, combine the granulated sugar, eggs, heavy cream, Calvados, vanilla, and salt and whisk until smooth. Pour the mixture into the tart shell to surround the apples, and bake for 40 to 45 minutes, or until the pastry is golden brown. Transfer to a wire rack to cool.

4. Dust with powdered sugar and sprinkle with lightly toasted sliced almonds before serving.

FOR THE PÂTE SABLÉE

2 cups (250 g) all-purpose flour, plus additional for dusting

½ cup (60 g) powdered sugar

Pinch of fine sea salt

8 tablespoons (1 stick/113 g) unsalted butter, cold and cubed, plus additional for greasing

1 large egg

FOR THE APPLE FILLING

3 medium apples, such as Granny Smith, Jonagold, and Braeburn

6 tablespoons (75 g) granulated sugar

2 large eggs

1 cup (240 ml) heavy cream

2 tablespoons (30 ml) Calvados

½ teaspoon (2.5 ml) pure vanilla extract

Pinch of fine sea salt

Powdered sugar, for dusting

¼ cup (24 g) lightly toasted sliced almonds, for sprinkling

mirabelle upside-down cake

The mirabelle plum is so popular in France that the northeastern city of Metz created an annual festival dedicated solely to celebrating these tiny golden fruits. At the end of August and in early September, mirabelle tarts become ubiquitous throughout the boulangeries of Paris, and mirabelle jam makes its way onto everyone's morning tartine. In fact, it was while I was heaping an extravagant amount of mirabelle jam onto toast one morning at Coutume on the Rive Gauche that the vision for this jammy cake came into focus. An upside-down cake allows the plums to caramelize together with brown sugar, cinnamon, and lots of butter, creating an irresistible sticky plum topping. I like to serve each slice with a generous dollop of crème fraîche, but whipped cream would work nicely, too.

SERVES 8 TO 10

MAKE THE PLUMS

1. Preheat the oven to 350°F (175°C). Grease and line a 9-inch (23-cm) round cake pan with parchment paper; set aside.

2. In a small bowl, whisk together the melted butter, dark brown sugar, cinnamon, and salt. Spread the mixture evenly on the bottom of the prepared pan. Arrange the mirabelles, cut side down, in an even layer. Fit as many plums as you can into the pan without overlapping.

MAKE THE CAKE

1. In a medium bowl, whisk together the flour, baking powder, baking soda, and salt. Set aside.

2. In a small bowl, whisk together the crème fraîche and milk; set aside.

3. In the bowl of a stand mixer fitted with the paddle attachment, beat the butter and granulated sugar together on medium-high until pale and fluffy, about 4 minutes. With the mixer on low, add the eggs, one at a time, scraping down the bowl with a rubber spatula between additions. Add the vanilla and mix until combined. Add the flour mixture in three additions, alternating with the crème fraîche mixture, mixing until just combined.

4. Using a rubber spatula, scrape the batter into the cake pan and gently spread to evenly cover the plums. Bake for 50 to 55 minutes, or until a cake tester inserted into the center comes out clean and the cake is golden brown. Transfer the cake to a wire rack to cool for 20 minutes before inverting the cake onto a cake stand or plate. Serve warm with a hearty dollop of crème fraîche.

FOR THE PLUMS

¼ cup (½ stick/56 g) unsalted butter, melted, plus additional for greasing

½ cup (110 g) firmly packed dark brown sugar

½ teaspoon (1 g) ground cinnamon

Pinch of fine sea salt

12 to 15 mirabelle plums, halved and pitted (see Note)

FOR THE CAKE

1¼ cups plus 3 tablespoons (181 g) all-purpose flour

1 teaspoon (4 g) baking powder

½ teaspoon (2 g) baking soda

½ teaspoon (2.5 g) fine sea salt

4½ ounces (126 g) crème fraîche, plus additional for serving

2 tablespoons (30 ml) whole milk

¾ cup (1½ sticks/170 g) unsalted butter, room temperature

½ cup (100 g) granulated sugar

2 large eggs, room temperature

2 teaspoons (10 ml) pure vanilla extract

Note: If you are unable to find mirabelles, Reine Claude or Italian prune plums would also work well in this recipe. You might need fewer of another varietal, as mirabelles are quite a small variety of plum—adjust the quantity as needed to ensure the plums fit snugly in the cake pan.

louise bonne galette

Galettes are probably my husband's favorite dessert. He loves their rustic, no-frills simplicity and flaky dough layered with butter. The recipe is a straightforward one: Just pick your favorite pear and gently tuck it into the folds of the dough before baking. We are spoiled for choice at the markets in Paris when it comes to pear selection in autumn. One of the prettiest is the Louise Bonne, a variety characterized by its beautiful coloring of yellow and green with a bright red flush. It's a richly flavored and juicy pear that I find bakes well in pies and cakes, but if you can't find any Louise Bonne, then Bosc or Bartlett pears work just as well. The spicy sugar mixture includes ground cloves, nutmeg, ginger, black pepper, and cinnamon, giving the pears a nice heat that balances well with the sugar. I tend to serve this galette warm straight from the oven while the pears are still bubbling away in the fragrant, caramelized sugar. SERVES 6

MAKE THE GALETTE DOUGH

1. In a food processor, pulse the flour, granulated sugar, and salt until combined. Add the cubes of butter and pulse until the mixture resembles coarse sand. Add 2 tablespoons (30 ml) of the ice-cold water and pulse about 4 times, or until the dough is crumbly in texture but holds together when squeezed—be careful not to overmix the dough. If the dough is still dry, add the remaining 1 tablespoon (15 ml) ice water and pulse to incorporate. Remove the dough from the food processor, flatten into a disc, wrap in plastic wrap, and refrigerate at least 1 hour or overnight.

2. Preheat the oven to 400°F (200°C). Line a baking tray with parchment paper or a silicone baking mat.

3. Remove the dough from the refrigerator 30 minutes before you plan to roll it out. Transfer the dough to a lightly floured work surface and roll out to a 12- to 14-inch (30- to 36-cm) round or oval—the dough should be about ⅛ inch (3 mm) thick. Carefully roll the dough around the rolling pin, brushing off any excess flour, then unroll the dough onto the prepared baking tray. Transfer the tray to the refrigerator while you prepare the filling.

FOR THE GALETTE DOUGH

1⅓ cups (167 g) all-purpose flour, plus additional for dusting

1 tablespoon (12.5 g) granulated sugar

¼ teaspoon (1 g) fine sea salt

¾ cup (1½ sticks/170 g) unsalted butter, cold and cubed

3 tablespoons (45 ml) ice-cold water

FOR THE PEAR FILLING

½ cup (100 g) granulated sugar

1 teaspoon (2 g) freshly ground black pepper

1 teaspoon (2 g) ground cinnamon

1 teaspoon (2 g) ground ginger

½ teaspoon (1 g) freshly grated nutmeg

¼ teaspoon (0.5 g) ground cloves

¼ teaspoon (1 g) fine sea salt

4 medium Louise Bonne or Bosc pears

1 tablespoon (15 ml) heavy cream

1 to 2 tablespoons (12.5 to 25 g) turbinado sugar

Crème fraîche or vanilla ice cream, for serving

MAKE THE PEAR FILLING

1. In a small bowl, combine the granulated sugar, pepper, cinnamon, ginger, nutmeg, cloves, and salt. Set aside.

2. Cut the pears in half lengthwise and remove the cores. Cut each half lengthwise into slices—cut all the way through the pears but keep the slices together so they still form a half.

3. Remove the galette dough from the refrigerator and arrange the pear halves in the center, fanning the halves out to cover the galette but leaving a 2-inch (5-cm) border around the edge. Sprinkle the sugar mixture over the pears, using your fingers to gently separate the slices to get some of the sugar in between the slices. Fold the border of the dough up and over the pears, folding and overlapping it to ensure the pears are snug. Brush the exposed dough with the heavy cream and sprinkle with turbinado sugar. Bake for 25 to 30 minutes, or until the crust is golden brown. Serve warm with a dollop of crème fraîche or vanilla ice cream.

blooms in my basket: l'automne

At fall markets, floral options wind down a bit after the summertime bounty. But there's still a range of breathtaking blooms to bring home as the leaves float down from overhead.

DAHLIAS. Always my autumn go-to. I buy these versatile flowers in all kinds of colors throughout the season. I particularly prefer the larger, more bodacious blooms with heads that droop down in dramatic fashion.

HYDRANGEAS: Called *hortensia* in French, an arrangement of soft, timeless hydrangeas makes an elegant impression with little effort. A simple bouquet in one color will do wonders for any room.

SUNFLOWERS. Joyful and confident, sunflowers warm up your home as the weather gets chillier. I keep an eye out for the showstopping double-flowered variety, made famous in the nineteenth-century bouquets painted by Vincent van Gogh.

JAPANESE MAPLE. The best way to bring the bold beauty of the outside in? Select a sky-high bunch of Japanese maple branches. With their fiery red leaves and tall, slender shapes, they offer a quick way to turn up the volume on your at-home flower arranging.

NOTE: Steer clear of autumn's chrysanthemums if you're bringing a bouquet to a friend in France, where they associate the voluminous bloom with death. In fact, it's the traditional flower you'll see placed on the final resting spots of loved ones on the Fête de la Toussaint, or All Saints' Day, on November 1 in notable Paris cemeteries such as Père Lachaise, Montparnasse, and Montmartre.

gâteau opéra

The first time I laid eyes on Paris's glorious opera house, Opéra Garnier, I felt mesmerized by the opulence, the drama of the sculpted faces peering from every corner, and, of course, its literary history. It's no wonder a cake equally as decadent was named in its honor. The gâteau opéra was first introduced to Parisians in 1955 by the Dalloyau pastry shop. Its rectangular shape was credited to head pastry chef Cyrique Gavillon and it was his wife, Andrée Gavillon, who allegedly gave it the name after exclaiming it reminded her of the famed opera's lavish stage. The sublime pairing of coffee and chocolate was an instant success, and versions can still be found in every pastry shop in France. Since I'm an aficionado of all things coffee-flavored, I had to include my own version here. The almond cake layers are soaked in a coffee syrup, then wrapped in espresso buttercream with ganache filling. This cake smells like a cup of freshly roasted joe—which, by the way, is the perfect pairing with a generous slice!

Note: A classic opera cake often incorporates edible gold leaf to give it a touch of that Garnier glamour—and I'm always excited to use it in my cake decorating. A little goes a long way, so while it may be enticing to gold leaf the entire cake, I'd use it sparingly. SERVES 10 TO 12

MAKE THE CHOCOLATE SHARDS

1. Place the finely chopped dark chocolate in a microwave-safe bowl and heat in 30-second increments, stirring occasionally, until melted, or use the double-boiler method (see Note, page 44).

2. Lay a sheet of parchment paper on a clean work surface. Using an offset palette knife, spread a thin, even layer of chocolate in a rectangle on the parchment. Place a second piece of parchment paper directly on top and smooth out using your hands. Starting with the edge of the parchment closest to you, roll the chocolate into a tight tube. Refrigerate until ready to use, at least 30 minutes.

MAKE THE ALMOND CAKE

1. Preheat the oven to 350°F (175°C). Grease and line three 6-inch (15-cm) round cake pans with parchment paper. Grease and flour the parchment paper. Set aside.

2. In a medium bowl, whisk together the flour, almond flour, baking powder, and salt; set aside.

FOR THE CHOCOLATE SHARDS

8 ounces (225 g) 70% dark chocolate, finely chopped

FOR THE ALMOND CAKE

¾ cup (1½ sticks/170 g) unsalted butter, room temperature, plus additional for greasing

1¾ cups (220 g) all-purpose flour, plus additional for dusting

½ cup (56 g) almond flour

2¼ teaspoons (9 g) baking powder

¾ teaspoon (3.5 g) fine sea salt

1½ cups (300 g) granulated sugar

3 large eggs

1½ teaspoons (7.5 ml) pure vanilla extract

1 cup (240 ml) buttermilk

FOR THE COFFEE SYRUP

1 cup (200 g) granulated sugar

1 cup (240 ml) strong brewed coffee

FOR THE ESPRESSO BUTTERCREAM

2 cups (4 sticks/450 g) unsalted butter, room temperature

5 cups (625 g) powdered sugar

¼ cup (60 ml) heavy cream

4 teaspoons (8 g) instant espresso powder

CONTINUED FROM PAGE 122

3. In the bowl of a stand mixer fitted with the paddle attachment, beat the butter and granulated sugar together until pale and fluffy, about 4 minutes. With the mixer on low, add the eggs, one at a time, scraping the bowl down with a rubber spatula between additions. Add the vanilla and mix to combine. Add the flour mixture in three additions, alternating with the buttermilk and mixing well after each addition.

4. Divide the batter among the prepared pans and bake for 30 to 35 minutes, or until a cake tester inserted into the centers comes out clean and the cakes are golden brown. Transfer the cakes to a wire rack to cool for 15 minutes before removing from the pans to cool completely.

MAKE THE COFFEE SYRUP

In a medium saucepan, combine the granulated sugar and coffee. Bring to a boil, stirring constantly to help dissolve the sugar. Once the sugar has dissolved, lower the heat and simmer, stirring occasionally, for 3 to 4 minutes. Transfer to a glass jar or other container and let cool completely.

MAKE THE ESPRESSO BUTTERCREAM

1. In the bowl of a stand mixer fitted with the paddle attachment, beat the butter on medium-high until pale and fluffy, about 4 minutes. Lower the speed and slowly add the powdered sugar, mixing well.

2. In a small bowl, combine the heavy cream and espresso powder and whisk to dissolve the espresso powder. Gradually add to the butter mixture, 1 tablespoon (15 ml) at a time, and mix well after each addition. Beat on high until fully combined and fluffy, 4 to 5 minutes.

MAKE THE CHOCOLATE GANACHE

1. Place the finely chopped bittersweet chocolate in a small heatproof bowl.

2. In a small saucepan set over medium heat, bring the heavy cream just to a boil. Pour the hot cream over the chocolate and let stand for 2 minutes, then stir until the chocolate is smooth and melted. Allow to cool and thicken before using.

ASSEMBLY

1. Using a serrated knife, level the cakes by trimming off the tops. Spread a small spoonful of buttercream onto the center of a cake stand or plate to secure the cake, and place the first cake layer directly on top. Lightly brush the top of the cake with a little coffee syrup. Transfer about a third of the buttercream to a piping bag fitted with a medium round pastry tip and pipe a circle of buttercream around the top outer edge of

FOR THE CHOCOLATE GANACHE

9 ounces (252 g) 65% bittersweet chocolate, finely chopped

1 cup plus 2 tablespoons (270 ml) heavy cream

FOR THE ASSEMBLY

Edible gold leaf (optional)

the cake layer. Spread about a third of the ganache in the center of the buttercream circle. Place the second cake layer on top and repeat the process with the coffee syrup, buttercream, and ganache. Place the final cake layer on top.

2. Use some of the remaining buttercream to spread a thin layer on the sides and top of the cake, then transfer to the refrigerator to allow the crumb coat to set, about 20 minutes.

3. Cover the sides and top of the cake in an even layer with the remaining buttercream.

4. Unroll the parchment-wrapped roll of chocolate—the chocolate will break into shards—and gently press the chocolate shards around the sides of the cake as desired.

5. Place the remaining ganache in a piping bag fitted with a medium French star pastry tip and pipe dollops around the top outer edge of the cake. Apply edible gold leaf to each dollop, if desired.

apple cardamom tea cake

While apple and cinnamon will always be an iconic pairing, I have more recently found the fragrance and subtlety of cardamom to be equally enticing and a great pairing with apples as well. This tea cake is studded with cardamom-flecked apple pieces and finished off with a tangy apple-cider glaze. I like to bake this cake using Granny Smith apples for their tartness and ability to hold their shape after baking. SERVES 9

MAKE THE APPLE CHIPS

1. Preheat oven to 225°F (105°C). Line baking tray with parchment paper.

2. Use a small sharp knife to cut the apple as thinly as possible, then place the apple slices in a single layer on the prepared baking tray. Sprinkle with the cinnamon. Bake for 60 minutes, then flip the slices over and bake for an additional 60 minutes.

MAKE THE TEA CAKE

1. Preheat the oven to 350°F (175°C). Grease and flour a 9-x-5-inch (23-x-12.5-cm) loaf pan; set aside.

2. In the bowl of a stand mixer fitted with the paddle attachment, beat the butter and granulated sugar together on medium-high until pale and fluffy, about 4 minutes. Add the oil, baking powder, cardamom, cinnamon, and salt, and beat until smooth and fluffy, 4 to 5 minutes. With the mixer on low, add the eggs, one at a time, and mix well after each addition. With the mixer on low, add the flour in two additions, alternating with the applesauce, and mix until just combined. Using a rubber spatula, scrape down the sides of the bowl then fold in the diced apples.

3. Pour the batter into the prepared loaf pan and bake for 55 to 60 minutes, or until a cake tester inserted into the center comes out clean and the cake is golden brown. Transfer the cake to a wire rack to cool for 10 minutes before removing from the pan to cool completely.

MAKE THE GLAZE

1. Meanwhile, in a small bowl, whisk together the powdered sugar, melted butter, and apple cider until well combined and smooth. Add more apple cider as needed to create a thick but pourable glaze.

2. Place a sheet of parchment paper underneath the rack holding the cooled cake. Starting at one end, pour the glaze over the cake, letting it drip down the sides. Decorate with the apple chips. Allow the glaze to set at room temperature for about 15 minutes before serving.

FOR THE APPLE CHIPS

1 apple, any variety

½ teaspoon (1 g) ground cinnamon

FOR THE TEA CAKE

8 tablespoons (1 stick/113 g) unsalted butter, room temperature, plus additional for greasing

2¾ cups plus 2 tablespoons (360 g) all-purpose flour, plus additional for dusting

1¾ cups (350 g) granulated sugar

½ cup (120 ml) sunflower oil

2 teaspoons (8 g) baking powder

1 teaspoon (2 g) ground green cardamom

1 teaspoon (2 g) ground cinnamon

1 teaspoon (4.5 g) fine sea salt

4 large eggs

½ cup (125 g) unsweetened applesauce

3 cups (340 g) peeled, cored, and diced apples (about 2 apples)

FOR THE GLAZE

1 cup (125 g) powdered sugar

2 tablespoons (28 g) unsalted butter, melted

1 tablespoon (15 ml) apple cider, plus additional as needed

fallen fig cake

This rustic fig cake comes together rather quickly, making it a good option to bake in the morning for a fabulous fall brunch. I love the simplicity of what I like to call a fallen fruit cake—cakes baked with a fresh fruit topping (see Fallen Apricot Pistachio Cake on page 79) as it allows the seasonal fruit flavor to shine—in this case, ripe figs. Fig season in France usually starts at the end of August, but it's in September and October when they come into full bloom and the market stalls heave with the full spectrum of fig varieties. Here, I use black mission figs, which I find add the perfect amount of sweetness. I usually like to sprinkle a bit of lightly toasted almond slices on this cake right before serving. SERVES 8 TO 10

1. Preheat the oven to 350°F (175°C). Grease and flour a 9-inch (23-cm) round cake pan; set aside.

2. In the bowl of a stand mixer fitted with the paddle attachment, beat the butter and light brown sugar together on medium-high until fluffy, about 4 minutes. Add the eggs, one at a time, mixing well after each addition. Add the vanilla and orange zest and beat until just combined.

3. In a medium bowl, whisk together the flour, baking powder, and salt. With the mixer on low, add the flour in three additions, alternating with the buttermilk, and mix until just combined.

4. Pour the batter into the prepared pan. Arrange the figs, cut side up, in a circular pattern and sprinkle with the granulated sugar. Bake for 55 to 60 minutes, or until a cake tester inserted into the center comes out clean and the cake is golden brown. Transfer the cake to a wire rack to cool for 10 minutes before carefully inverting onto the rack. Sprinkle with sliced almonds and serve warm with crème fraîche.

¾ cup (1½ sticks/170 g) unsalted butter, room temperature, plus additional for greasing

2 cups (250 g) all-purpose flour, plus additional for dusting

1⅓ cups (295 g) firmly packed light brown sugar

2 large eggs, room temperature

2 teaspoons (10 ml) pure vanilla extract

1 tablespoon (6 g) grated orange zest

1½ teaspoons (6 g) baking powder

¼ teaspoon (1 g) fine sea salt

1 cup (240 ml) buttermilk

10 to 12 small ripe figs, cut in half

2 tablespoons (25 g) granulated sugar

¼ cup (24 g) lightly toasted sliced almonds

Crème fraîche, for serving

persimmon bundt cake

Persimmons start appearing toward the end of autumn and can be found at the markets through December. I keep an eye out for the Fuyu variety, which resemble squat, plump tomatoes. During this time of year, I store plenty of them around the house in old compotiers, bowls with a pedestal designed specifically for displaying fresh fruit. When ripe, they have a sweet pudding-like interior that makes for a very moelleux, or soft, cake. I've found they taste best in this type of cake when slightly overripe. Serve it dusted with powdered sugar or toast a slice, then top with a pat of salted butter, as you would with banana bread. SERVES 12

8 tablespoons (1 stick/113 g) salted butter, melted, plus additional for greasing

3 cups plus 1 tablespoon (383 g) all-purpose flour, plus additional for dusting

1¾ cups (350 g) granulated sugar

1 teaspoon (4 g) baking soda

1 teaspoon (2 g) ground cinnamon

½ teaspoon (1 g) ground nutmeg

½ teaspoon (2.5 g) fine sea salt

½ cup (120 ml) sunflower oil

2 very ripe Fuyu persimmons, peeled and cut in half

3 large eggs, room temperature

Powdered sugar, for dusting

1. Preheat the oven to 325°F (165°C). Grease and flour a 10- to 12-cup (2.4- to 2.8-L) Bundt pan, or use baking spray; set aside.

2. In a large bowl, whisk together the flour, granulated sugar, baking soda, cinnamon, nutmeg, and salt. Add the melted butter, oil, and the flesh from the persimmons, and stir to combine. Add the eggs, one at a time, mixing well after each addition.

3. Pour the batter into the prepared pan and bake for 55 to 60 minutes, or until a cake tester inserted into the center of the cake comes out clean—the cake will rise and get firm on top. Transfer the cake to a wire rack to cool for 10 minutes before carefully removing from the pan to cool completely. Dust with powdered sugar just before serving.

praliné all day cake

As a seasoned pastry and chocolate guide for visitors to our city, I can safely say I've tried vast quantities of Parisian chocolate. Within all the wonderful varieties and flavor combinations, though, I'm consistently drawn to the praliné noisette, or hazelnut butter wrapped in chocolate (not to be confused with the cream-based praline confection of the American South). Chocolatier Alain Ducasse on rue Saint-Benoît houses the most divine collection of praliné chocolates that I'd be happy to eat for the rest of my life. Whenever I take a new group of tasters to the shop, I always recommend they try his almond or hazelnut praliné . . . and then I stand back to witness the rapture and revelation that inevitably follows. This cake, featuring hazelnut cake layers filled with praliné and wrapped in silky chocolate meringue frosting, is for all my fellow praliné lovers who could eat praliné literally all day. I like to decorate it with a crown of hazelnuts from Piedmont, Italy, considered the best in the world. You can try making your own praliné for the filling or simply use it as an excuse to plan your next trip to Paris to source a jar directly at Alain Ducasse! SERVES 12

MAKE THE HAZELNUT CAKE

1. Preheat the oven to 350°F (175°C). Grease and line two 8-inch (20 cm) round cake pans with parchment paper. Grease and flour the parchment paper. Set aside.

2. In a medium bowl, whisk together the flour, ground hazelnuts, baking powder, and salt.

3. In a small bowl whisk together the eggs, egg yolks, buttermilk, and hazelnut extract. Set aside.

4. In the bowl of a stand mixer fitted with the paddle attachment, beat the butter on medium-high until pale and fluffy, about 4 minutes. With the mixer on low, gradually add the granulated sugar, ½ cup at a time. Once all the sugar has been added, turn the mixer up to medium-high and beat until pale and fluffy, about 5 minutes. Reduce the speed to low and add the flour mixture in three additions, alternating with the buttermilk mixture, and mix until just combined. Turn off the mixer and give the batter one more mix, using a rubber spatula to scrape down the bowl completely.

5. Divide the batter evenly among the prepared pans and bake for 45 to 50 minutes, or until a cake tester inserted into the centers comes out clean and the cakes are golden brown. Transfer the cakes to a wire rack to cool for 10 minutes before removing from the pans to cool completely.

FOR THE HAZELNUT CAKE

1 cup (224 g) unsalted butter, room temperature, plus additional for greasing

4 cups (550 g) all-purpose flour

½ cup (38 g) ground hazelnuts

3¼ teaspoon baking powder

½ teaspoon fine sea salt

2 cups (400 g) granulated sugar

4 large eggs plus 2 egg yolks, room temperature

2 teaspoons (10 ml) hazelnut or vanilla extract

1½ cups (330 g) buttermilk, room temperature

FOR THE CHOCOLATE BUTTERCREAM

6 ounces (170 g) 70% dark chocolate, finely chopped

1 cup (200 g) granulated sugar

4 large egg whites

2 cups (4 sticks/450 g) unsalted butter, room temperature

FOR THE ASSEMBLY

1 cup (240 ml) Hazelnut & Almond Praliné (page 135 or store-bought)

½ cup (60 g) whole hazelnuts, plus ⅓ cup (28 g) finely chopped hazelnuts

CONTINUED FROM PAGE 133

MAKE THE CHOCOLATE BUTTERCREAM

1. Place the finely chopped dark chocolate in a microwave-safe bowl and heat in 30-second increments, stirring occasionally, until melted, or use the double-boiler method (see Note, page 44). Set aside to cool.

2. Combine the granulated sugar and 1/4 cup (60 ml) water in a small saucepan set over high heat. Bring to a boil and continue cooking until the syrup reaches soft-ball stage, or 240°F (115°C) on a candy thermometer, 8 to 10 minutes.

3. Meanwhile, in the bowl of a stand mixer fitted with the whisk attachment, whip the egg whites on high until stiff peaks form.

4. Once the syrup has reached 240°F (115°C), carefully pour it into the egg white mixture in a slow steady stream with the mixer on low. Once all the syrup has been added, turn the mixer up to high and whisk until cool, about 5 minutes.

5. With the mixer set to medium-high, add the butter, 1 tablespoon (14 g) at a time, until fully combined. Once all the butter has been added, turn the mixer back up to high and beat until smooth and fluffy, about 4 minutes. Turn the mixer down to low and add the melted chocolate, then mix on high for 2 to 3 minutes, or until smooth and fluffy.

ASSEMBLY

1. Using a serrated knife, level the cakes by trimming off the tops, then split the cakes in half horizontally so you have 4 layers. Spread a small spoonful of buttercream onto the center of a cake plate or stand to secure the cake and place the first cake layer directly on top. Transfer about a third of the buttercream to a piping bag fitted with a medium round pastry tip. Pipe a ring around the top outer edge of the cake, then fill the center with about ⅓ of the praliné. Place the second cake layer on top and repeat the process.

2. Place the last cake layer on top and use an offset palette knife to spread a thin layer of buttercream around the sides and top of the cake. Transfer the cake to the refrigerator to allow the crumb coat to set, about 15 minutes.

3. Cover the sides and top of the cake with the remaining buttercream.

4. Decorate the cake with a ring of whole hazelnuts on top and gently press crushed hazelnuts around the base of the cake.

hazelnut & almond praliné

In most French pantries, you'll find praliné—a delicious spread made with caramel and either roasted hazelnuts or almonds, or, as in the case of this recipe, both. It's a popular breakfast staple enjoyed on top of a toasted baguette called a tartine . . . though I know many people who admit to eating spoonfuls of it directly from the jar. It's also used as a filling in chocolates and sometimes in cakes, as in my Praliné All Day Cake (page 133). This keeps in a jar in the fridge for up to a month, though it rarely lasts that long at my house! MAKES 18 OUNCES (500 G)

9 ounces (255 g) hazelnuts

9 ounces (255 g) almonds

1¼ cups (250 g) granulated sugar

1 tablespoon (15 ml) pure vanilla extract

Pinch of fine sea salt

1. Preheat the oven to 350°F (175°C). Line a baking tray with parchment paper or a silicone baking mat.

2. Place the hazelnuts and almonds on the prepared baking tray and roast for about 20 minutes, or until golden brown and fragrant. Transfer the nuts to a plate and set aside to cool; reserve the prepared baking tray.

3. Place the granulated sugar in a saucepan set over medium heat and cook, without stirring, until melted and golden brown. Once the sugar has caramelized, turn off the heat, add the cooled hazelnuts and almonds, and stir with a wooden spoon to evenly coat the nuts with the caramel. Transfer to the prepared baking tray and allow to cool, 5 to 10 minutes.

4. In a food processor or blender, combine the caramelized nuts with the vanilla and salt. Pulse until the mixture resembles a nut butter, about 5 minutes. Transfer to a mason jar and store, covered in the refrigerator, for up to 1 week.

quatre quart with roasted plums

Quatre Quart, or "four fourths," is a pound cake in which all four ingredients are of roughly equal weight. It's a sublime cake that you can bake into one large loaf or individual mini loaves, and lends itself to a variety of add-ins like chocolate, berries, or seasonal fruits, such as pears and apples. I enjoy it plain with fresh berries in summer or, as in this autumn version, with petite roasted plums known as prune bleue or quetsche. I'm always delighted to see their deep purple pop up in market stalls around the end of August and on through to October. They are extremely delicious when roasted in the oven with your favorite fall spices (think cinnamon, clove, and cardamom). Preparing them this way also creates a pretty pink syrup that I spoon onto bowls of Greek yogurt or porridge and serve alongside this buttery cake.

If you don't have prune bleue or quetsche where you are, prune plums make a nice substitute. SERVES 6 TO 9, DEPENDING ON THE PAN

FOR THE CAKES

1 cup (225 g) unsalted butter, melted, plus additional for greasing

2 cups (250 g) all-purpose flour, plus additional for dusting

1 cup (200 g) granulated sugar

4 large eggs

2 teaspoons (10 ml) pure vanilla extract

Grated zest of 1 lemon

1 teaspoon (4.5 g) fine sea salt

FOR THE ROASTED PLUMS

25 ounces (709 g) prune plums (10 to 12 small plums), halved and pitted

2 tablespoons (28 g) unsalted butter, melted

2 tablespoons (25 g) granulated sugar

Grated zest of 1 orange

1 teaspoon (2 g) ground cinnamon

¼ cup (60 ml) freshly squeezed orange juice

MAKE THE CAKES

1. Preheat the oven to 350°F (175°C). Grease and flour 6 mini loaf pans or a 9-x-5-inch (23-x-12.5-cm) loaf pan; set aside.

2. In a medium bowl, whisk together the melted butter and granulated sugar. Add the eggs, one at a time, whisking well after each addition. Add the vanilla, lemon zest, and salt, and mix until just combined. Gradually add the flour in small increments, and mix until just combined.

3. Pour the batter into the prepared pans or pan and bake until a cake tester inserted into the center comes out clean and the cake is golden brown, 25 to 30 minutes if baking mini loaves, or 55 to 60 minutes if using a single loaf pan. Transfer to a wire rack to cool for 10 minutes before removing from the pans or pan to cool completely.

MAKE THE ROASTED PLUMS

1. Preheat the oven to 375°F (190°C).

2. Place the plums, cut side up, in a baking dish large enough to fit them all in a single layer. Brush the plums with the melted butter then sprinkle with granulated sugar, orange zest, and cinnamon. Drizzle the orange juice over the plums. Cover the baking dish with aluminum foil and bake for 20 to 30 minutes, or until the plums are tender.

3. Serve the cakes or cake with the roasted plums and sauce. (Leftover plums and sauce can be stored in the refrigerator, covered, for up to one week.)

pear spice cake

Poached fruit? Yes, please! For me, pears are one of the tastiest fruits when poached with spices, wine, or honey. In this compote, they're cooked down with vanilla bean, making for a delicious cake filling. I've made this spice cake often for my fall cake-decorating workshops to rave reviews. Its warm ginger notes balance beautifully with the sweetness of the pear filling . . . and everyone knows brown butter frosting, with its fragrant and nutty taste, just makes everything better. SERVES 8 TO 10

MAKE THE CAKE

1. Preheat the oven to 350°F (175°C). Grease and line three 6-inch (15-cm) round cake pans with parchment paper. Grease and flour the parchment paper. Set aside.

2. In a large bowl, whisk together the flour, baking powder, baking soda, cinnamon, ginger, nutmeg, cloves, and salt; set aside.

3. In a medium bowl, whisk together the oil, dark brown sugar, applesauce, eggs, and vanilla. Add to the flour mixture and whisk until combined.

4. Divide the batter among the prepared pans and bake for 35 to 40 minutes, or until a cake tester inserted in the centers comes out clean and the cakes are golden brown. Transfer the cakes to a wire rack to cool for 10 minutes before removing from the pans to cool completely.

MAKE THE PEAR-VANILLA BEAN COMPOTE

Place the pears in a medium saucepan. Using the tip of a sharp knife, scrape the seeds from the vanilla bean into the pan. Add the light brown sugar, lemon juice, and cinnamon stick. Bring to a gentle boil over medium-high heat, stirring until the sugar is dissolved. Reduce the heat to medium-low and continue cooking, uncovered and stirring occasionally, for an additional 20 to 25 minutes, or until the compote is golden. Remove from the heat, add the butter, and stir until incorporated. Remove the cinnamon stick and transfer the compote to a jar or glass container. The compote can be stored in the refrigerator, covered, until ready to use.

MAKE THE BEURRE NOISETTE BUTTERCREAM

1. In a medium saucepan set over medium heat, melt the butter and cook until fragrant and amber brown, 8 to 10 minutes. Transfer immediately to a heatproof bowl and let cool at room temperature for 15 minutes. Cover with plastic wrap and transfer to the refrigerator to chill until firm, about 1 hour, stirring periodically to prevent separation.

FOR THE CAKE

Unsalted butter, for greasing

2½ cups (315 g) all-purpose flour, plus additional for dusting

2 teaspoons (8 g) baking powder

1 teaspoon (4 g) baking soda

1½ teaspoons (3 g) ground cinnamon

1 teaspoon (2 g) ground ginger

½ teaspoon (1 g) ground nutmeg

½ teaspoon (1 g) ground cloves

½ teaspoon (2.5 g) fine sea salt

1 cup (240 ml) sunflower oil

1¾ cups plus 4 teaspoons (403 g) firmly packed dark brown sugar

¾ cup (185 g) unsweetened applesauce

4 large eggs

2 teaspoons (10 ml) pure vanilla extract

FOR THE PEAR-VANILLA BEAN COMPOTE

4 large pears, ideally Bosc or Anjou, peeled, cored, and diced

1 vanilla bean, split lengthwise *(see page 73 for vanilla bean note)*

½ cup (110 g) firmly packed light brown sugar

Freshly squeezed juice of 1 lemon

1 cinnamon stick

1 tablespoon (14 g) unsalted butter

2. Remove the butter from the refrigerator and let stand at room temperature for a few minutes, then place in the bowl of a stand mixer fitted with the paddle attachment, and beat on high until fluffy, 4 to 5 minutes. Reduce the speed to low and gradually add the powdered sugar, 1 cup (125 g) at a time. Use a rubber spatula to scrape down the bowl between additions. Add the heavy cream and vanilla and beat on high until smooth, 4 to 5 minutes.

ASSEMBLY

1. Using a serrated knife, level the cakes by trimming off the tops. Spread a small spoonful of buttercream onto the center of a cake plate or stand to secure the cake, and place the first cake layer directly on top. Transfer about a third of the buttercream to a piping bag fitted with a medium round pastry tip. Pipe a ring around the top outer edge of the cake and fill with about ¼ cup (60 ml) of the pear–vanilla bean compote. Place the second cake layer on top and repeat the process. Place the last cake layer on top.

2. Use an offset palette knife to spread a thin layer of buttercream over the sides and top of the cake. Transfer the cake to the refrigerator to allow the crumb coat to set, about 20 minutes.

3. Cover the sides and top of the cake with the remaining buttercream. Decorate the top of the cake with miniature pears, figs, and dahlias.

FOR THE BEURRE NOISETTE BUTTERCREAM

2 cups (4 sticks/450 g) unsalted butter

5 cups (625 g) powdered sugar

1 tablespoon (15 ml) heavy cream

1 teaspoon (5 ml) pure vanilla extract

FOR THE ASSEMBLY

2 miniature pears, for decorating

2 figs, for decorating

2 to 3 small dahlias, for decorating

caramel beurre salé cake

This cake has become one of my signatures; almost everybody I know in Paris has requested it at some point or another. In fact, whenever I see her around the building, Madame Seco, our gardienne (the French term for landlady or building caretaker), has even taken to asking me when I'll be making the "gateau deluxe," as she calls it! I love its decadent combination of dark chocolate cake layers, salted caramel filling (caramel au beurre salé), and fluffy caramel frosting. I usually sprinkle even more flaky shards of fleur de sel between the layers, as it tends to heighten that addictive salty/sweet note. SERVES 10 TO 12

MAKE THE CHOCOLATE CAKE

1. Preheat the oven to 350°F (175°C). Grease and line three 6-inch (15-cm) round cake pans with parchment paper. Grease and flour the parchment. Set aside.

2. In a medium bowl, whisk together the flour, granulated sugar, cocoa powder, baking powder, baking soda, and salt. Gradually add the hot coffee in a slow steady stream, whisking continuously until combined. Add the buttermilk and mix until combined. Add the oil and mix until combined. Add the eggs, one at a time, mixing well after each addition. Add the vanilla and mix until smooth.

3. Divide the batter evenly among the prepared pans and bake for 30 to 35 minutes, or until a cake tester inserted into the centers comes out clean— the cakes will crack and be firm on top. Transfer the cakes to a wire rack to cool for 10 minutes before removing from the pans to cool completely.

MAKE THE SALTED CARAMEL BUTTERCREAM

1. In a small saucepan set over high heat, combine the granulated sugar and ¼ cup (60 ml) water. Bring to a boil and continue cooking until the syrup reaches soft-ball stage, or 240°F (115°C) on a candy thermometer, 8 to 10 minutes.

2. Meanwhile, in the bowl of a stand mixer fitted with the whisk attachment, whisk the egg whites on high until stiff peaks form.

3. Once the sugar syrup has reached 240°F (115°C), carefully pour it into the egg whites in a slow steady stream with the mixer on low. Once all the syrup has been added, turn the mixer up to high and whisk until cooled, about 5 minutes.

FOR THE CHOCOLATE CAKE

Unsalted butter, for greasing

2⅓ cups (292 g) all-purpose flour, plus additional for dusting

2 cups (400 g) granulated sugar

½ cup (50 g) Dutch-process cocoa powder

2 teaspoons (8 g) baking powder

2 teaspoons (8 g) baking soda

½ teaspoon (2.5 g) fine sea salt

1 cup (240 ml) brewed coffee, hot

1 cup (240 ml) buttermilk

½ cup (120 ml) sunflower oil

2 large eggs, room temperature

1½ teaspoons (7.5 ml) pure vanilla extract

FOR THE SALTED CARAMEL BUTTERCREAM

1 cup (200 g) granulated sugar

4 large egg whites

2 cups (4 sticks/450 g) unsalted butter, room temperature

½ cup (120 ml) salted caramel, room temperature

FOR THE CHOCOLATE CURLS

4 ounces (113 g) 70% dark chocolate, finely chopped

2 teaspoons (9 g) butter, room temperature

FOR THE ASSEMBLY

1 cup (240 ml) salted caramel, room temperature

1 recipe dark chocolate shards (see page 122)

4. With the mixer at medium-high speed, add the butter, 1 tablespoon (14 g) at a time, until fully combined. Once all the butter has been added, whip on high until light and fluffy, 4 to 5 minutes more. With the mixer off, add the salted caramel, then turn the mixer back up to medium-high and mix until smooth.

MAKE THE CHOCOLATE CURLS

1. In a microwave-safe bowl, combine the finely chopped dark chocolate and the butter. Microwave in 30-second increments, stirring occasionally, until melted, or use the double-boiler method (see Note, page 44). Pour the melted chocolate onto the back of a clean baking tray and use an offset palette knife to spread it into a thin, even layer that covers most of the tray. Transfer the baking tray to the refrigerator and allow the chocolate to set, 30 to 45 minutes.

2. Carefully and slowly drag a bench scraper or metal spatula from one end of the chocolate to the other to create curls. If the chocolate softens, return the tray to the refrigerator for 5 to 10 minutes. Transfer the chocolate curls to a plate and refrigerate until ready to use.

ASSEMBLY

1. Using a serrated knife, level the cakes by trimming off the tops. Spread a small spoonful of buttercream onto the cake plate or stand to secure the cake and place the first cake layer directly on top. Transfer about a third of the buttercream to a piping bag fitted with a medium French star pastry tip and set aside for decorating. Transfer another third of the buttercream to a piping bag fitted with a medium round pastry tip and pipe a circle around the top outer edge of the cake. Fill the circle with about ½ cup (120 ml) salted caramel and spread it evenly within the circle. Place the second cake layer on top and repeat the process. Place the last cake layer on top.

2. Using an offset palette knife, spread a thin layer of buttercream around the sides and top of the cake. Transfer the cake to the refrigerator to allow the crumb coat to set, about 20 minutes.

3. Cover the sides and top of the cake completely using the remaining buttercream.

4. Use the reserved piping bag of buttercream to pipe dollops in a border around the top edge of the cake. Place a chocolate curl on each dollop then gently press chocolate shards along the bottom of the cake.

chapter 4

l'hiver

{ winter }

WHEN OUR PLANE touched down on the day we moved to Paris, in January 2012, my sunny Californian heart melted. White blanketed the entire city. Paris was a snow extravaganza.

It was a moment I'd been preparing for my whole life. Despite growing up in San Diego, a city without winter—without changing seasons at all—I was a guy with an extensive knitwear collection. I'd often get teased for how many sweaters I would wear ("You're seriously sporting another cardigan, Frank?") but I knew what I was doing.

I was dressing for a season I wished I lived in.

With flakes dancing overhead and thick snow crunching underfoot, I trekked with James and our dog, Parker—each layered in excellent knitwear, bien sûr—to the Luxembourg Gardens to take it all in. The water in the fountains had iced over in dramatic fashion, while snow nestled into the curves of frozen statues and dusted the lofty seventeenth-century roof of Marie de Médicis's Luxembourg Palace like powdered sugar.

Here we were, walking in a winter wonderland. It was the kind of old-world magic that Hollywood films had promised me. Our cheeks were nice and rosy and Jack Frost nipped at all manner of noses. Chestnuts were actually being roasted by street vendors on an open fire close by, filling the air with a warm, nutty toastiness. People sat packed together under cozy blankets on Parisian terraces on the Île Saint-Louis, sipping warmly spiced wine called vin chaud and mugs of hot chocolate.

Through the years, I'd come to learn that, while occasional flurries will visit for an hour or two and then disappear just as fast, snowstorms here are rare. My dreamy introduction to winter in Paris was a fluke. Gray, overcast, and chilly, this season in the city is less "Let It Snow!" and more "A Hazy Shade of Winter." As the French would say, the weather is moche, ugly, and a tad gloomy, especially during the long months of January and February, when the gray is so unending that you can't even see the sky.

Paris being Paris, however, it still manages to dazzle.

There are plenty of ways the City of Light keeps you warm, even on the most moche of days. For me, winter signals the start of museum season. While gallery hopping is great all year round, this is the time I seek relief from the cold in my favorite art institutions. There's nothing cozier than an afternoon of getting lost among the world-class paintings and sculptures in places like the Rodin Museum, the Gustave Moreau Museum, the Musée d'Orsay, or the Musée Guimet.

Around mid-November, traditional Christmas markets also appear, enticing long, meandering strolls through Saint-Germain-des-Prés or the Champs-Élysées, vin chaud in hand, warming both the heart and the head. Closer to the holidays, lavish lights go up in place Vendôme, where it's easy to wander down from its well-appointed shops to rue Saint-Honoré, where you can peek at festive store windows, all while sneaking into your coat pocket for another bite (or two) of marron glacé, the coveted candied chestnuts that come out only at this time of year.

It's one of the season's most highly anticipated treats. But it is certainly not the only one.

Once the first hint of cold wind drifts down rues and up avenues, conversations with friends over coffee—often focused on food, because this is France—turn to pastry. And also, because this is France, opinions on wintertime creations are strong. In December, you're likely to hear

"You absolutely must try the bûche de Noël by this pastry chef" or "Did you know she's actually attempting to make her own bûche for Christmas dinner?" Come January, the month of Epiphany, the gossip turns to the reigning galette des rois, the classic king's cake filled with a lucky fève figurine. "Oh my God, did you try the insane galette at that boulangerie with a new black sesame filling?" is just as likely to be heard as "Oh my God, can you *believe* the insane galette at that boulangerie didn't use a traditional frangipane filling?"

As deliciously divisive as pastry can be, there is one thing Parisians do agree on: the comfort we still find in our neighborhood markets in the wintertime. Like this season's shorter, colder days, the marchés become darker and a bit less colorful. At my local market on boulevard Richard-Lenoir, I find different richly hued mushrooms, a variety of nuts, from beautiful chestnuts to walnuts in thick shells, and neat rows of plump, sticky medjool dates that will end up as mini medjool date cakes served with orange caramel sauce (see page 166). Deep jewel tones line the aisles compliments of everything from beets and parsnips to endive, cabbage, and cauliflower. However, all bets are off once citrus arrives on the scene—and a zesty parade of bright color wakes up the surrounding stalls, in a kaleidoscope of clementines, mandarins, blood oranges, lemons, and pink grapefruit. I immediately start imagining who I'd invite over to share sweet blood orange cakes (see page 169) with, or a slice of brûléed Lemon Meringue Cake (page 159).

Even for a California boy who always wanted a winter, this shot of citrusy sunshine is a welcome change from days of endless gray. And it's these winter fruits you'll often find filling my bag when I'm in the mood to bake. Hours later, you'd no doubt spot me settled in for an at-home goûter, a festive slice of Chestnut Cake (page 173) in hand or a favorite biscuit, like the jam-filled linzer (see page 189), balancing on the saucer under my teacup. The dog's at my feet, a captivating novel is nearby, and always, without question, I'm cozied into a sweater and ready for winter, snowflakes or not.

blooms in my basket: l'hiver

There is a surprisingly lovely selection of flowers for the taking at Paris's winter markets—
all offering bright spots for the season's longer, colder days.

MIMOSA. A giant vase filled with sunshine-yellow mimosa? Get ready for instant happiness in your home (especially as they come out right when the season is at its darkest and dreariest). The golden star of wintertime on the Côte d'Azur, it's a simple bloom that doesn't need any other frills to create a stunning bouquet.

RANUNCULUS. A rival to the rose, these winter beauties add refinement and romance to any space—no surprise, as these are considered the flower of seduction. Long-lasting and robust, ranunculus comes in a range of colors from white to shades of pink.

ANEMONES. I often buy these in bulk, as I adore the contrast between the dark, moody center and the delicate but dramatic petals. I prefer to stick to the one-color rule with anemone bouquets, too—it keeps things looking chic.

WINTER BONUS: CITRUS MOMENTS. Here in France, markets sell the highly coveted Corsican clementines with their feuilles, or green leaves, attached, making for a dramatic wintry arrangement when piled high in beautiful bowls. To make your own, use whatever winter citrus you can find at your local market!

white chocolate & cassis bûche de noël

Baker beware: This recipe is not for the faint-hearted. The Swiss roll cake is a deceptively simple-looking cake; however, the technique of pre-rolling and then rolling the cake back out again to fill it nearly conquered me the first time I attempted it. A bûche de Noël is an absolute Christmastime must on every French holiday table, whether purchased or painstakingly produced by hand. Over the years we've tried almost every flavor imaginable, as all the pastry chefs in Paris find clever new ways to assemble and fill their bûche logs, spheres, and cubes with everything from yuzu compote to coffee-infused mousselines. For my recipe, I chose cassis, or black currant, jam for its tartness, which I find to be the perfect complement to the sweet white-chocolate buttercream, fluffy mascarpone whipped cream, and white chocolate bark. Charming chocolate-dipped meringue mushrooms and sugared cranberries complete this festive dessert. Since there are so many components you can add to your bûche de Noël, it's a cake best prepared in parts over two or three days before the big day. And don't fret if your bûche isn't picture-perfect—it's a holiday dessert that's meant to be charming, and it will still leave your friends and family asking for seconds. SERVES 8 TO 10

MAKE THE MERINGUE MUSHROOMS

1. Preheat the oven to 400°F (200°C).

2. Line a baking tray with parchment paper, spread the superfine sugar on top, and bake for 7 minutes.

3. Meanwhile, in the bowl of a stand mixer fitted with the whisk attachment, combine the egg whites and salt. Whisk the egg whites beginning on low and gradually moving to high until stiff peaks form.

4. Take the sugar out of the oven and turn the oven down to 225°F (105°C). With the mixer on medium-high, gradually spoon the hot sugar into the egg white mixture, making sure it's fully incorporated between additions. Once all the sugar has been added, add the vanilla and mix to incorporate, then continue mixing on high until the mixture is smooth and glossy, about 5 minutes. Line a baking tray with a fresh sheet of parchment paper.

5. Transfer the meringue mixture to a piping bag fitted with a medium round pastry tip. Pipe 1-inch (2.5-cm) mounds directly onto a piece of parchment paper to form the caps of the mushrooms, then pipe 1-inch (2.5-cm) lines for the stems. Using the back of a spoon dipped in water, flatten any peaks that might have formed so the mushrooms are smooth.

FOR THE MERINGUE MUSHROOMS

1½ cups (300 g) superfine sugar

5½ ounces (154 g) egg whites (approximately 4 large egg whites)

½ teaspoon (2.5 g) fine sea salt

½ teaspoon (2.5 ml) pure vanilla extract

2 tablespoons (13 g) Dutch-process cocoa powder

3 ounces (84 g) 65% bittersweet chocolate, finely chopped

FOR THE WHITE CHOCOLATE BARK

8 ounces (225 g) white chocolate, finely chopped

FOR THE CAKE

¼ cup (½ stick/56 g) unsalted butter, melted, plus additional for greasing

¾ cup (94 g) all-purpose flour, plus additional for dusting

4 large eggs, separated

⅔ cup (135 g) granulated sugar

1 teaspoon (5 ml) pure vanilla extract

1 teaspoon (4 g) baking powder

¼ teaspoon (1 g) fine sea salt

2 tablespoons (15 g) powdered sugar

½ cup (160 g) cassis (black currant) jam

CONTINUED FROM PAGE 153

Place the cocoa powder in a small sifter and dust the meringue mushrooms with cocoa powder. Bake 45 minutes to 1 hour, or until the parchment paper easily peels off the meringues. Turn off the oven and leave the meringues to dry out in the oven for several hours or overnight.

6. Place the finely chopped bittersweet chocolate in a microwave-safe bowl and heat in 30-second increments, stirring occasionally, until melted, or use the double-boiler method (see Note, page 44). Set aside to cool.

7. Using the tip of a paring knife, carefully cut small holes, about the size of the mushroom stems, in the undersides of the meringue mushroom caps. Working with one mushroom at a time, dip the underside of a cap and the tip of a stem in the melted chocolate, then gently push the stem into the hole in the cap, allowing the chocolate to act as edible glue. Place on a piece of parchment paper and allow to set. (You can keep the mushrooms uncovered in the freezer until ready to use.)

MAKE THE WHITE CHOCOLATE BARK
1. Place the finely chopped white chocolate in a microwave-safe bowl and heat in 30-second increments, stirring occasionally, until melted, or use the double-boiler method. Set aside to cool.

2. Lay a sheet of parchment paper on a clean work surface. Using an offset palette knife, spread a thin, even layer of chocolate in a rectangle on the parchment. Place a second piece of parchment paper directly on top and smooth out using your hands. Starting with the edge of the parchment closest to you, roll the chocolate into a tight tube. Refrigerate until ready to use, at least 60 minutes.

MAKE THE CAKE
1. Preheat the oven to 350°F (175°C). Grease and line a 12 x 17-inch (30-x-43-cm) baking pan with parchment paper. Grease and flour the parchment paper. Set aside.

2. In the bowl of a stand mixer fitted with the whisk attachment, combine the egg whites with ⅓ cup (68 g) of the granulated sugar and beat on high until stiff peaks form, about 5 minutes.

3. In a small bowl, combine the egg yolks, the remaining ⅓ cup (68 g) granulated sugar, and vanilla and whisk until pale and creamy.

4. In a large bowl, sift together the flour, baking powder, and salt.

FOR THE MASCARPONE WHIPPED CREAM
1¼ cups (300 ml) heavy cream, cold

¾ cup (90 g) powdered sugar

1 teaspoon (5 ml) pure vanilla extract

8 ounces (225 g) mascarpone cheese

FOR THE WHITE CHOCOLATE MERINGUE BUTTERCREAM
7 ounces (200 g) white chocolate, finely chopped

1 cup (200 g) granulated sugar

4 large egg whites

2 cups (4 sticks/450 g) unsalted butter, room temperature

FOR THE ASSEMBLY
Powdered sugar, for dusting

About 1 cup (100 g) sugared cranberries and currants (optional; see page 84)

Ground pistachios (optional)

5. Pour the melted butter and egg yolk mixture over the flour mixture and whisk until completely combined. Using a rubber spatula, gently fold in the egg whites until fully incorporated; the batter will be very light. Spread the batter evenly in the prepared pan and bake for 10 to 12 minutes, or until the top of the cake gently springs back when touched. Be careful not to overbake. Clean the stand mixer bowl and whisk attachment and place in the refrigerator to chill for at least 30 minutes before making the mascarpone whipped cream.

6. While the cake is baking, place a thin tea towel flat on a clean work surface and dust the entire surface with the powdered sugar.

7. Once the cake comes out of the oven, let it cool on a wire rack for just 1 minute before inverting it onto the powdered sugar–dusted tea towel. Leave the parchment paper in place. Starting at one short end, gently roll the cake and tea towel up to the other short end. Allow the cake to cool, rolled in the tea towel and seam side down, for about 20 minutes. Don't leave the cake for too long, as it should still be slightly warm when it's time to unroll it.

MAKE THE MASCARPONE WHIPPED CREAM

1. Meanwhile, in the chilled bowl of a stand mixer fitted with the chilled whisk attachment, whip the heavy cream, powdered sugar, and vanilla on medium-high until stiff peaks form.

2. Add the mascarpone cheese and whip until stiff peaks form again.

3. Slowly and gently unroll the cake and remove the parchment paper. Spread the cassis jam evenly on top, leaving about a ½-inch (1-cm) border around the edges. Spread the mascarpone whipped cream directly on top of the jam layer.

4. Gently roll the cake back up, without the tea towel, then refrigerate, seam side down, while you make the buttercream.

MAKE THE WHITE CHOCOLATE MERINGUE BUTTERCREAM

1. Place the finely chopped white chocolate in a microwave-safe bowl and heat in 30-second increments, stirring occasionally, until melted, or use the double-boiler method (see Note, page 44). Set aside to cool.

2. Combine the granulated sugar and ¼ cup (60 ml) water in a small saucepan set over high heat. Bring to a boil and continue cooking until the syrup reaches soft-ball stage, or 240°F (115°C) on a candy thermometer, 8 to 10 minutes.

CONTINUED FROM PAGE 155

3. Meanwhile, in the bowl of a stand mixer fitted with the whisk attachment, whisk the egg whites on high until stiff peaks form.

4. Once the syrup has reached 240°F (115°C), carefully pour it into the egg white mixture in a slow steady stream with the mixer on low. Once all the syrup has been added, turn the mixer up to high and whisk until cool, about 5 minutes.

5. With the mixer set to medium-high, add the butter, 1 tablespoon (14 g) at a time, until fully combined. Once all the butter has been added, mix on high until fully combined. Add the melted white chocolate and mix until light and fluffy, 4 to 5 minutes.

ASSEMBLY

1. Remove the cake roll from the refrigerator and place on a cake plate or server. Use an offset palette knife to spread the buttercream over the top and sides of the cake roll. Using a sharp knife, trim both end pieces off the cake roll to reveal the inside swirl at both ends.

2. Unroll the parchment-wrapped roll of chocolate—the chocolate will break into shards—and place the shards lengthwise along the top and sides of the cake. Refrigerate for 30 to 60 minutes.

3. Lightly dust the cake with powdered sugar to resemble fallen snow. Decorate with festive sugared cranberries and currants, if using, and spoon ground pistachios around the base to resemble moss, if desired. Add the meringue mushrooms on both sides in small groupings and voilà, your bûche de Noël is ready to take center stage on your holiday table.

Notes: Make the meringue mushrooms the day before; they will keep fresh in the freezer until you are ready to use them. I also like to place a bowl of the mushrooms on my table alongside the finished bûche so everyone gets one on their plate.

Before you begin the cake itself, make the white chocolate bark and set it aside in the refrigerator until it's ready to use. If you'd like to skip the bark, you can use an offset palette knife to draw lines into the bûche by lightly dragging the tip of the palette knife across the cake from one end to the other to resemble bark on a log.

lemon meringue cake
(gâteau au citron)

Who doesn't love an excuse to break out the kitchen torch and brûler something delicious? This lemon meringue cake celebrates the flavors of a tarte au citron without the pastry base. It's inspired in part by the over-the-top tarte au citron found at a small hidden-away café in the Marais called Le Loir dans la Théière, which loosely translates to "The Dormouse in the Teapot." They make a lemon tart topped with a fluffy mile-high meringue that's toasted to perfection. My ideal wintertime afternoon would include cozying up with a steaming pot of tea and a big slice of this. My cake is filled with tart lemon curd and wrapped in meringue, which, when torched, smells just like roasted marshmallow. I recommend making the lemon curd the day before, so it has time to set in the fridge overnight before being added to your cake layers. Leftover lemon curd makes a great topping for yogurt and tastes excellent sandwiched between shortbread. SERVES 10 TO 12

MAKE THE LEMON CURD

1. In a medium saucepan off the heat, whisk together the eggs and granulated sugar, then set over medium heat and cook, whisking continuously, until the sugar is fully dissolved and the mixture is fully combined, 2 to 3 minutes. Add the lemon zest, lemon juice, and salt and whisk until fully incorporated, about 1 minute. Gradually add the cubes of butter, one at a time, whisking well after each addition. Lower the heat slightly and continue cooking, stirring occasionally, until the curd starts to thicken, about 4 minutes.

2. Once the curd is smooth and thick, remove from the heat and pour through a fine-mesh strainer set over a bowl. Discard any solids. Allow the curd to cool to room temperature, about 20 minutes, then cover with plastic wrap, pressing it directly onto the surface of the curd to prevent a skin forming. Refrigerate until cold and set, at least several hours and preferably overnight.

MAKE THE LEMON CAKE

1. Preheat the oven to 350°F (175°C). Grease and line four 6-inch (15-cm) round cake pans with parchment paper. Butter and flour the parchment paper. Set aside.

2. In a food processor, combine the sugar and lemon zest and process on high for 3 to 4 minutes, or until well combined; set aside.

3. In a large bowl, whisk together the flour, baking powder, baking soda, and salt; set aside.

FOR THE LEMON CURD

4 large eggs

1 cup (200 g) granulated sugar

2 tablespoons (12 g) grated lemon zest (from about 2 lemons)

¾ cup (180 ml) freshly squeezed lemon juice (from about 3 lemons)

⅛ teaspoon (.5 g) fine sea salt

8 tablespoons (1 stick/113 g) unsalted butter, cut into cubes

FOR THE LEMON CAKE

1 cup (2 sticks/225 g) unsalted butter, room temperature, plus additional for greasing

2¾ cups (344 g) all-purpose flour, plus additional for dusting

2 cups (400 g) granulated sugar

1 tablespoon (6 g) grated lemon zest (from about 1 lemon)

2½ teaspoons (10 g) baking powder

½ teaspoon (2 g) baking soda

½ teaspoon (2.5 g) fine sea salt

3 large eggs, room temperature

1 cup (240 ml) buttermilk

⅓ cup (80 ml) freshly squeezed lemon juice (from about 2 lemons)

FOR THE MERINGUE

1 cup (200 g) granulated sugar

4 large egg whites

CONTINUED FROM PAGE 159

4. In the bowl of a stand mixer fitted with the paddle attachment, beat the butter and lemon sugar together on medium-high until pale and fluffy, about 4 minutes. With the mixer on low, add the eggs, one at a time, scraping down the bowl using a rubber spatula after each addition. With the mixer on low, add about a third of the flour mixture, followed by the buttermilk. Add another third of the flour mixture, followed by the lemon juice. Add the remaining flour mixture and mix until just combined, being careful not to overmix. Scrape down the bowl with a rubber spatula one final time.

5. Divide the batter evenly among the prepared pans and bake 30 to 35 minutes, or until a cake tester inserted into the centers comes out clean and the cakes are golden brown. Transfer the cakes to a wire rack to cool for 15 minutes before removing from the pans to cool completely.

MAKE THE MERINGUE

1. Combine the granulated sugar and ¼ cup (60 ml) water in a small saucepan set over high heat. Bring to a boil and continue cooking until the syrup reaches the soft-ball stage, or 240°F (115°C) on a candy thermometer, 8 to 10 minutes.

2. Meanwhile, in the bowl of a stand mixer fitted with the whisk attachment, whisk the egg whites on high until stiff peaks form.

3. Once the syrup has reached 240°F (115°C), carefully pour it into the egg whites in a slow steady stream with the mixer on low. Once all the syrup has been added, turn the mixer up to high and whisk until cool, about 5 minutes.

ASSEMBLY

1. Using a serrated knife, level the cakes by trimming off the tops. Spread a small spoonful of meringue onto the center of a cake stand or plate to secure the cake, and place the first cake layer directly on top. Transfer a little more than a third of the meringue to a piping bag fitted with a medium round pastry tip and pipe a circle on the top outer edge of the cake. Fill the center with about ¼ cup (60 ml) of the lemon curd, being sure to stay within the border of the meringue circle. Top with the second cake layer and repeat the process two more times. Place the fourth and final cake layer on top.

2. Using an offset palette knife, spread the remaining meringue over the sides and top of the cake, creating swirls as you go. If desired, use the back of a spoon to create more dramatic swoops and swirls on the surface of the cake. Using a kitchen torch, brûler the entire cake as bien cuit, or well-cooked, as you like—start slowly, as you can always go back over the cake to give it more color.

gâteau orangette

One of the many treats you will always see in a French chocolatier is the beloved orangette, a candied orange peel that's been dipped in dark or milk chocolate. Nowadays you can also find candied ginger, grapefruit, and lemon amongst the chocolatey confections on offer, but orange remains the most prized. One of my favorite iterations comes from Patrick Roger, a sleek and avant-garde chocolate house on place Saint-Sulpice, whose orangette is certainly one of the most generous in terms of size I've seen in Paris. My loaf cake finds inspiration in that bitter and sweet combination, with bright orange zest baked directly into the chocolate cake and a luxuriously thick chocolate glaze finished with slices of homemade candied orange (best made the day before) as decor. To dial up the orange flavor in the cake, you can also add diced candied orange to the batter—add it in last and fold in with a rubber spatula. It lends texture to this cake and is a great way to use up extra candied orange slices. SERVES 8 TO 10

MAKE THE CANDIED ORANGE SLICES

1. Wash the orange, cut off and discard both end pieces, and then cut into 6 crosswise slices and remove any seeds. Fill a bowl with ice water.

2. Bring a medium pot of water to a boil, add the orange slices, and blanch for 2 minutes. Drain and transfer the slices to the ice water. Drain again.

3. In a saucepan large enough to fit the orange slices in a single layer, combine the granulated sugar and ½ cup (120 ml),water over medium heat. Cook, stirring occasionally, until the sugar dissolves completely. Lower the heat to a simmer, add the orange slices in a single layer, and simmer on low, turning the orange slices every 15 minutes, until the skins turn translucent, about 1 hour. Using tongs, transfer the orange slices to a piece of parchment paper set on a wire rack and let cool overnight.

4. The next day, sprinkle the orange slices with coarse sugar for a sparkly finish or leave as is. Cut a slice in half and set aside for decorating the cake. Dice two slices and set aside for adding to the batter, if using. Reserve any remaining orange slices for another use.

MAKE THE CHOCOLATE ORANGE CAKE

1. Preheat the oven to 350°F (175°C). Grease and line a 9-x-5-inch (23-x-12.5-cm) loaf pan with parchment paper, covering the bottom and long sides of the pan and leaving a 1-inch (2.5-cm) overhang on both sides. Set aside.

FOR THE CANDIED ORANGE SLICES

1 medium navel orange

½ cup (100 g) granulated sugar

Coarse sugar (optional)

FOR THE CHOCOLATE ORANGE CAKE

8 tablespoons (1 stick/113 g) unsalted butter, room temperature, plus additional for greasing

1¼ cups (157 g) all-purpose flour, plus additional for dusting

⅔ cup (66 g) Dutch-process cocoa powder

1 teaspoon (4 g) baking soda

¼ teaspoon (1 g) baking powder

¾ teaspoon (3.5 g) fine sea salt

1½ cups (300 g) granulated sugar

3 large eggs, room temperature

2 teaspoons (10 ml) pure vanilla extract

1 tablespoon (6 g) grated orange zest

¾ cup (180 g) buttermilk

FOR THE CHOCOLATE GLAZE

6 tablespoons (84 g) unsalted butter

¼ cup (60 ml) heavy cream, plus additional as needed

¼ cup (25 g) Dutch-process cocoa powder

2 cups (250 g) powdered sugar

CONTINUED FROM PAGE 162

2. In a medium bowl, whisk together the flour, cocoa powder, baking soda, baking powder, and salt; set aside.

3. In the bowl of a stand mixer fitted with the paddle attachment, beat the butter and granulated sugar together until pale and fluffy, about 4 minutes. With the mixer on low, add the eggs, one at a time, and mix until combined, scraping down the bowl with a rubber spatula between each addition. Add the vanilla and orange zest, and mix until just combined. Add the flour mixture in three additions, alternating with the buttermilk, and mix until just combined. Use a rubber spatula to make sure everything is well mixed. Fold in the diced candied orange with a rubber spatula, if using.

4. Transfer the batter to the prepared pan. Bake for 60 minutes, or until a cake tester inserted into the center of the cake comes out clean—the cake will rise and crack on top. Transfer the cake to a wire rack to cool for 10 minutes before using the parchment paper overhang to lift the cake out of the pan. Return the cake to the wire rack to cool completely.

MAKE THE CHOCOLATE GLAZE

1. Meanwhile, melt the butter in a small saucepan set over low heat. Add the heavy cream and cocoa powder and cook, whisking, until the mixture thickens.

2. Remove from heat, then gradually add the powdered sugar in batches, and whisk until well combined and smooth. Add a splash more cream as needed to create a thick but pourable glaze. Keep warm.

ASSEMBLY

1. Place a sheet of parchment paper underneath the rack holding the cooled cake. Starting at one end, pour the glaze over the cake, letting it drip down the sides and going back and forth from one end to the other to completely cover the cake.

2. Decorate the cake with the candied orange slices. Allow the glaze to set at room temperature for about 15 minutes before serving.

medjool date cakes
in orange caramel sauce

I've been obsessed with medjool dates ever since trying them on my first visit to Marrakech, where they were served alongside a tall, cold glass of orange blossom–infused almond milk. When ripe, medjool dates have a rich and caramel-like taste and can be used in a variety of ways. With a texture that reminds me of sticky toffee pudding, these cakes are the perfect winter treat! SERVES 6

MAKE THE MEDJOOL DATE CAKES

1. Preheat the oven to 350°F (175°C). Grease and flour 6 mini Bundt pans or use baking spray; set aside.

2. Place the dates and baking soda in a large bowl. In a small saucepan, heat the milk over medium heat until just boiling. Pour the hot milk over the dates and let sit for 10 minutes, then mash everything together; set aside.

3. In a medium bowl, whisk together the flour, baking powder, and salt.

4. In the bowl of a stand mixer fitted with the paddle attachment, beat the butter and dark brown sugar together until fluffy, about 4 minutes. Add the eggs, one at a time, mixing well after each addition. With the stand mixer on low, add the flour mixture, and mix until fully combined. Add the date mixture and mix until well combined. Using a rubber spatula, scrape down the sides of the bowl and give the batter one last mix.

5. Divide the batter evenly among the prepared pans and bake for 30 to 35 minutes, or until a cake tester comes out clean and the cakes are golden brown. Transfer the cakes to a wire rack to cool for 5 minutes before carefully removing from the pans to cool completely.

MAKE THE ORANGE CARAMEL SAUCE

1. Meanwhile, in a medium saucepan set over medium heat, stir together the orange juice and granulated sugar using a wooden spoon. Carefully watch the mixture, without stirring, until it begins to turn dark amber.

2. Remove from the heat, add the heavy cream and butter, and stir until smooth. Stir in the fleur de sel.

3. Place the mini Bundt cakes on individual plates and pour the caramel directly into the center of each one, letting it spill slightly over the edges and pool around the base of the cake.

FOR THE MEDJOOL DATE CAKES

6 tablespoons (84 g) unsalted butter, room temperature, plus additional for greasing

1½ cups (189 g) all-purpose flour, plus additional for dusting

10 ounces (280 g) pitted medjool dates

1 teaspoon (4 g) baking soda

1 cup (240 ml) whole milk

1½ teaspoons (6 g) baking powder

Pinch of fine sea salt

3 tablespoons (42 g) firmly packed dark brown sugar

2 large eggs

FOR THE ORANGE CARAMEL SAUCE

½ cup (120 ml) freshly squeezed orange juice (from about 3 oranges)

1½ cups (300 g) granulated sugar

½ cup (120 ml) heavy cream

2 tablespoons (28 g) unsalted butter

¼ teaspoon (1 g) fleur de sel or coarse sea salt

blood orange mini bundt cakes

I always look forward to spotting the striking color of blood oranges at the winter markets. Usually piled high amongst the rest of the winter citruses, they have a reddish blush to their skin and a deep, dark maroon interior. The juice creates the prettiest shade of pink in glazes or sauces and brings delectable notes of raspberry to the flavor. I think you'll agree that these bright and happy little cakes make the perfect antidote to the seemingly endless grisaille of January. MAKES 6 CAKES

MAKE THE BLOOD ORANGE CAKES

1. Preheat the oven to 350°F (175°C). Grease and flour 6 mini Bundt pans or use baking spray; set aside.

2. In a medium bowl, whisk together the flour, baking powder, and salt; set aside.

3. In a food processor, pulse together the granulated sugar and blood orange zest until well combined. Transfer to the bowl of a stand mixer fitted with the paddle attachment, add the butter, and beat together on medium-high until pale and fluffy, about 4 minutes. With the mixer on low, add the eggs, one at a time, scraping down the bowl with a rubber spatula between additions, and mix until well combined. Add about a third of the flour mixture, followed by the buttermilk. Add another third of the flour mixture, followed by the blood orange juice. Add the remaining flour mixture and mix until just combined. Be careful not to overmix.

4. Divide the batter evenly among the prepared pans and bake for 30 to 35 minutes, or until a cake tester comes out clean and the cakes are golden brown. Transfer the cakes to a wire rack to cool for 5 minutes before carefully removing from the pans to cool completely.

MAKE THE GLAZE

1. Meanwhile, in a small bowl, whisk together the powdered sugar and blood orange juice until well combined and smooth. Add more blood orange juice or powdered sugar as needed to create a thick but pourable glaze.

2. Place a sheet of parchment paper underneath the rack holding the cooled cakes. Pour enough glaze on each cake to allow it to drip down the sides. Allow the glaze to set at room temperature for about 15 minutes before serving.

FOR THE BLOOD ORANGE CAKES

1 cup (2 sticks/225 g) unsalted butter, room temperature, plus additional for greasing

3 cups plus 1 tablespoon (383 g) all-purpose flour, plus additional for dusting

1 tablespoon (12 g) baking powder

1 teaspoon (4.5 g) fine sea salt

2 cups (400 g) granulated sugar

½ cup (48 g) grated blood orange zest (from about 4 blood oranges)

4 large eggs, room temperature

1 cup (240 ml) buttermilk

¼ cup (60 ml) freshly squeezed blood orange juice (from about 1 blood orange)

FOR THE GLAZE

2 cups (250 g) powdered sugar, plus additional as needed

2 tablespoons (30 ml) freshly squeezed blood orange juice, plus additional as needed

alsatian gingerbread
(pain d'épices)

Since traditional French pain d'épices—or spice bread—is sweetened only with honey, you'll often spot loaves of this seasonal treat for sale at market stalls of miel merchants, piled high between jars of golden wildflower and amber buckwheat honeys. The spices vary by region, but the Alsatian variety most commonly uses star anise, giving the cake a fragrant note of licorice. The recipe also features dark rye flour, lending a bit of acidity. I like to dress up this loaf cake with a light orange liqueur glaze, but it's just as delicious when served plain. SERVES 9

MAKE THE CAKE

1. Preheat the oven to 350°F (175°C). Grease and flour a 9-x-5-inch (23-x-12.5-cm) loaf pan; set aside.

2. In a medium bowl, sift together the all-purpose flour, rye flour, baking soda, cinnamon, ginger, star anise, and salt; set aside.

3. In the bowl of a stand mixer fitted with the paddle attachment, beat the dark brown sugar, honey, eggs, and orange zest together until well combined. With the mixer on low, add the flour mixture in three additions, alternating with the milk and using a rubber spatula to scrape down the sides of the bowl between additions.

4. Transfer the batter to the prepared pan and bake 55 to 60 minutes, or until a cake tester inserted into the middle comes out clean and the cake is firm and golden on top. Transfer the cake to a wire rack to cool for 10 minutes before removing from the pan to cool completely.

MAKE THE ORANGE GLAZE (OPTIONAL)

1. Meanwhile, in a small bowl, whisk together the powdered sugar and orange liqueur until well combined and smooth. Add more powdered sugar or liqueur as needed to create a very thin glaze.

2. Place a sheet of parchment paper underneath the rack holding the cooled cake. Pour the glaze over the cooled cake, letting it drip down the sides, and going back and forth from one end to the other to completely cover the cake. Decorate with cinnamon sticks, star anise pods, and candied orange peel. Allow the glaze to set at room temperature for about 15 minutes before serving.

FOR THE CAKE

Unsalted butter, for greasing

1 cup (125 g) all-purpose flour, plus additional for dusting

1 cup (125 g) rye flour

2½ teaspoons (10 g) baking soda

1½ teaspoons (3 g) ground cinnamon

1½ teaspoons (3 g) ground ginger

1 teaspoon (2 g) freshly ground star anise

½ teaspoon (2 g) fine sea salt

3 tablespoons (42 g) firmly packed dark brown sugar

1 cup (240 ml) honey, ideally single varietal

2 large eggs, room temperature

1 tablespoon (6 g) grated orange zest (from 1 orange)

1 cup (240 ml) whole milk

FOR THE ORANGE GLAZE (OPTIONAL)

1 cup (125 g) powdered sugar, plus additional as needed

1 teaspoon (5 ml) orange liqueur or freshly squeezed orange juice, plus additional as needed

Cinnamon sticks, for decorating

Star anise pods, for decorating

Candied orange peel, for decorating

chestnut cake
(gâteau ardèchois)

The Ardèche region in southeastern France is blessed with an abundance of chestnut trees, giving way to countless recipes, both savory and sweet, using the prized and versatile nut. This chestnut cream cake has a pleasingly soft texture and earthy taste that's perfect for a holiday goûter served with chai or even as a wintertime breakfast with your morning coffee. As with most baking, using ingredients at room temperature allows them to more easily emulsify, which results in a fluffier cake. SERVES 10

MAKE THE CHESTNUT CAKE

1. Preheat the oven to 350°F (175°C). Grease and flour a 9-cup (2.1-L) Kouglof pan or a 10- to 12- cup (2.4- to 2.8-L) Bundt pan; set aside.

2. In a medium bowl, sift together the flour, baking powder, baking soda, and salt; set aside.

3. In the bowl of a stand mixer fitted with the whisk attachment, whisk together the eggs, granulated sugar, and light brown sugar until pale and well combined, about 4 minutes.

4. In a medium bowl, combine the crème de marron with the butter and use a rubber spatula to mix until fully combined. Add this mixture to the egg mixture and mix until smooth and combined. Add the flour mixture in three additions, scraping down the sides of the bowl in between additions. Make sure not to overmix; the batter should be light and fluffy.

5. Transfer the batter to the prepared pan and bake for 50 to 55 minutes, or until a cake tester inserted in the center comes out clean—the cake will crack and be firm on top. Transfer the cake to a wire rack to cool for 10 minutes before carefully removing from the pan to cool completely.

MAKE THE VANILLA GLAZE

1. Meanwhile, in a medium bowl, whisk together the powdered sugar, milk, and vanilla until well combined and smooth. Add more powdered sugar or milk as needed to create a thick but pourable glaze.

2. Set a sheet of parchment underneath the rack holding the cooled cake. Pour the glaze over the cake, letting it drip down the sides. Decorate with branches of sugared rosemary. Allow the glaze to set at room temperature for about 15 minutes before serving.

FOR THE CHESTNUT CAKE

1 cup (2 sticks/225 g) unsalted butter, room temperature or softened, plus additional for greasing

2 cups (250 g) all-purpose flour, plus additional for dusting

1 teaspoon (4 g) baking powder

1 teaspoon (4 g) baking soda

¼ teaspoon (1 g) fine sea salt

5 large eggs, room temperature

½ cup (100 g) granulated sugar

⅛ cup (25 g) packed light brown sugar

18 ounces (500 g) crème de marron (sweetened chestnut cream)

FOR THE VANILLA GLAZE

2¼ cups (280 g) powdered sugar, plus additional as needed

3 tablespoons (45 ml) whole milk, plus additional as needed

1 teaspoon (5 ml) pure vanilla extract or créme de châtaignes d'Ardèche

Sugared rosemary branches, for decorating (see page 84)

winter citrus cake

This one-tin cake is a bright and zesty confection that I love to bake in winter, when citrus season is in full swing. Since it's only one layer, there's no need to worry about any fancy stacking and filling. It's topped with a fluffy mascarpone cream infused with a splash of orange blossom water that reminds me of Morocco, where we like to occasionally escape to during the cold winter months. I like to decorate this cake with a few slices of candied clementines, physalis, and lovely little orange blossom flowers.

SERVES 8 TO 10

MAKE THE CAKE

1. Preheat the oven to 350°F (175°C). Grease and line a 9-inch (23-cm) springform pan with parchment paper.

2. In a medium bowl, combine the olive oil, milk, orange juice, eggs, and citrus zest. Whisk until well combined and set aside.

3. In a large bowl, whisk together the flour, salt, baking powder, baking soda, and sugar. Slowly add in the wet ingredients to mix everything together until well incorporated. Be careful not to overmix the batter.

4. Pour the batter into the prepared pan. Bake the cake for 45 to 50 minutes or until a cake tester or toothpick inserted into the center of the cake comes out clean. Transfer the cake to a wire rack to cool in the pan for 10 minutes before turning the cake out to cool completely before frosting.

MAKE THE ORANGE BLOSSOM MASCARPONE FROSTING

1. In the bowl of a stand mixer fitted with the whisk attachment, or using a handheld mixer, combine the heavy cream, powdered sugar, and orange blossom water. Whip on high speed until stiff peaks form. With the mixer set to low, add in the mascarpone and whip to combine on medium-high speed until stiff peaks re-form.

ASSEMBLY

Using an offset spatula, spread the mascarpone frosting on top of the cooled cake. Decorate with orange blossoms, candied citrus, and golden berries.

FOR THE CAKE

1 cup (240 ml) lemon olive oil

1¼ cups (300 g) whole milk

¼ cup (60 ml) freshly squeezed orange juice

3 large eggs, room temperature

1 tablespoon (6 g) bergamot orange zest or your favorite winter citrus (blood orange, Cara Cara)

2 cups (250g) all-purpose flour

1 teaspoon (4 g) fine sea salt

½ teaspoon (2 g) baking powder

½ teaspoon (2 g) baking soda

1¼ cups (250g) granulated sugar

FOR THE ORANGE BLOSSOM MASCARPONE FROSTING

1¼ cups (300 ml) heavy cream, cold

¾ cup (90 g) powdered sugar

1 teaspoon (5 ml) orange blossom water

8 ounces (225 g) mascarpone cheese

ASSEMBLY

Orange blossoms, for decorating

Candied citrus, for decorating

Golden berries, for decorating

must-not-miss winter experiences in paris

1) This is the right time to indulge in one of my favorite winter pastries, le Mont-Blanc. Although many pastry chefs create their own versions of the chestnut-covered meringue and whipped cream concoction, the original at the legendary Angelina tearoom is still my favorite.

2) Galette des rois season is upon us! Try your luck all January long to select the slice of the flaky frangipane-filled tart that contains a small fève, a unique (and some-times collectible) ceramic figurine that allows the winner to don a gold paper crown during dessert.

3) While wandering through a winter market, try marron glacé, France's storied candied chestnut, and sip a cup of fragrant vin chaud, a warm, mulled wine infused with spices, citrus, and a touch of dark brown sugar.

4) Take tea at a palace hotel (the Four Seasons George V and the Ritz Paris being my top two preferences). If you time it right, you can even try an individual bûche de Noël with your winter tea.

bon voyage biscuit box

This international biscuit box brings together a collection
of sweets I've enjoyed in various countries throughout my
travels. I believe one of the best ways to get to know another
culture is through its food—and more specifically, through its
baked goods! There's nothing I love more than researching
traditional sweets to try before traveling to a new place.
Those discoveries are sometimes happenstance, however,
like when your hotel offers you a plate of local biscuits with
tea and you experience wonderful flavors you're inspired to
re-create back home. When making your own holiday box—
a festive gift for friends and family—feel free to include as
many as you like, ensuring you have a variety of flavors,
shapes, and sizes. It might also be fun to include smaller treats
like candy canes, truffles (see page 211), or individually
wrapped marron glacé, as I did here.

matcha pinwheels

Although matcha is not a traditional holiday flavor, I just love using it in baking, because its earthy taste balances so well with sweeter pairings like vanilla and white chocolate. These buttery biscuits come together in a snap and look so festive as part of a holiday biscuit box. Be sure to use cooking-grade matcha powder here, which has a slightly more astringent flavor profile than ceremonial matcha, making it shine through when used in baking. A note on vanilla sugar: Vanilla sugar is a simple combination of granulated sugar infused with vanilla beans. You can either make a home-made version with these two ingredients or look for them sold in sachets in your local baking aisle of the grocery store. MAKES 30 COOKIES

2¼ cups (282 g) all-purpose flour

¼ teaspoon (1 g) fine sea salt

7 tablespoons (98 g) unsalted butter, room temperature

½ cup (60 g) powdered sugar

1 large egg, room temperature

1 tablespoon (12.5 g) vanilla sugar

2½ teaspoons (5 g) cooking-grade matcha powder

1. In a medium bowl, sift together the flour and salt; set aside.

2. In the bowl of a stand mixer fitted with the paddle attachment, beat the butter and powdered sugar together on medium-high until light and fluffy, about 4 minutes. With the mixer on low, add the egg and vanilla sugar, mix to combine, and then scrape down the bowl using a rubber spatula. Add the flour mixture and use a rubber spatula to mix until well combined.

3. Divide the dough in half, add matcha powder to one half, and mix until fully incorporated. Divide both halves of the dough in half again so you end up with two equal portions of vanilla dough and two equal portions of matcha dough.

4. On a lightly floured work surface, roll each portion of dough out to a roughly 8-x-10-inch (20-x-25-cm) rectangle. Place a matcha rectangle on top of a vanilla rectangle and use a rolling pin to gently press them together. Repeat with the other rectangles of vanilla and matcha dough. Starting with the shorter side, roll the rectangles of dough into logs. Tightly wrap the two logs in plastic wrap and refrigerate for at least 1 hour and preferably overnight.

5. Preheat the oven to 350°F (175°C). Line two baking trays with parchment paper or silicone baking mats.

6. Remove a cookie log from the refrigerator and let it warm up for a few minutes at room temperature. Using a sharp knife, cut each log into ¼-inch (5-mm) slices. Place on the prepared baking trays and bake for 10 to 12 minutes, or until golden. Slide the parchment paper or silicone mats onto wire racks and let the cookies cool completely. Repeat as needed with the remaining dough.

hallongrotta (raspberry caves)

I first tried these tiny little cookies in a charming bakery on the island of Gamla Stan, the historic center of Stockholm. They were the perfect bite of butter and jam, and I was told the Swedes have been enjoying them with their afternoon coffee since the 1800s! Americans know them as thumbprint cookies due to the technique of making an imprint or "cave" in the center with your thumb and filling it with jam. Note that these cookies are lightly baked and should not brown. Although raspberry jam is the classic flavor, you can substitute with any jam you like, or even use chocolate ganache or salted caramel. MAKES 25 COOKIES

1. Line two baking trays with parchment paper or silicone baking mats; set aside.

2. In a large bowl, whisk together the flour, powdered sugar, potato flour, vanilla sugar, baking powder, and salt. Add the butter and use your fingertips to rub it into the flour until a dough forms.

3. Using about a tablespoon and a half of dough per cookie, shape the dough into balls and place on the prepared baking trays. Using your thumb, create a small indent in the center of each ball.

4. Fill each cookie with a teaspoon (5 ml) of raspberry jam. Refrigerate at least 30 minutes or overnight.

5. Preheat the oven to 350°F (175°C). Bake the first tray of cookiess for 12 to 15 minutes, or until firm. Be careful not to overbake these cookies, as they are meant to be pale. Slide the parchment paper or silicone mats onto wire racks and let the cookies cool completely. Once the first batch of cookies are out of the oven, place the second tray of cookies in the oven and repeat the baking process.

2¼ cups (282 g) all-purpose flour

1 cup (125 g) powdered sugar

5½ tablespoons (50 g) potato flour

1 tablespoon (12.5 g) vanilla sugar (see page 181)

1 teaspoon (4 g) baking powder

¼ teaspoon (1 g) fine sea salt

14 tablespoons (1¾ sticks/200 g) unsalted butter, room temperature, cubed

½ cup plus 1 teaspoon (167 g) seedless raspberry jam

mexican wedding cookies

Buttery and nutty treats that resemble miniature snowballs thanks to a double dusting of powdered sugar, Mexican wedding cookies are one of my holiday baking staples. I like to use pure Mexican vanilla for its deep spicy-sweet character, which imparts a hint of clove and nutmeg in this delectable cookie. MAKES 30 COOKIES

1. In a medium bowl, whisk together the flour, cinnamon, and salt; set aside.

2. In the bowl of a stand mixer fitted with the paddle attachment, beat the butter and ½ cup (60 g) of the powdered sugar together until pale and fluffy, about 4 minutes. Add the vanilla and mix until well combined. With the mixer on low, gradually add the flour mixture in small batches, mixing well after each addition. Add the pecans and mix with a wooden spoon or rubber spatula until incorporated. Wrap the dough in plastic wrap and refrigerate at least 30 minutes or overnight.

3. Preheat the oven to 325°F (165°C). Line two baking trays with parchment paper or silicone baking mats. Place the remaining 1¾ cups (220 g) powdered sugar in a shallow bowl and set aside.

4. Roll the dough with your hands to form small balls, roughly 1¼ inches (3 cm) in diameter, and place onto the prepared baking trays. Refrigerate for 15 minutes, then bake for 12 to 16 minutes, or just until the bottoms are golden. Do not overbake. Transfer the baking trays to a wire rack and let cool for 5 minutes, then toss the cookies in powdered sugar and place back on the rack to cool completely. Once the cookies have cooled completely, toss in powdered sugar again. Repeat as needed with the remaining dough.

2 cups (250 g) all-purpose flour

½ teaspoon (1 g) ground cinnamon

¼ teaspoon (1 g) fine sea salt

1 cup (2 sticks/225 g) unsalted butter, room temperature

2¼ cups (280 g) powdered sugar

1 teaspoon (5 ml) pure Mexican vanilla extract

1 cup (115 g) finely chopped pecans, lightly roasted

écorces d'oranges au chocolat

In France, candied fruits remain a popular holiday tradition and are often given as celebratory gifts to friends and family. Candied orange slices dipped in chocolate are beloved for being both zesty and sugary. Dark chocolate complements the sweet-tart flavor of orange without over-whelming it. Candied oranges can also be used as garnishes for cakes, as in my Gâteau Orangette (page 162). Be sure to look for a juicing variety of orange, such as navel or Valencia, as thicker-skinned varieties don't work as well here. MAKES 12 SLICES

2 medium navel oranges

1 cup (200 g) granulated sugar

3¼ ounces (91 g) semisweet chocolate, finely chopped

1. Wash the oranges, cut off and discard the end pieces, and then cut each orange into 6 crosswise slices and remove any seeds. Fill a bowl with ice water.

2. Bring a large pot of water to a boil, add the orange slices, and blanch for about 2 minutes. Drain and transfer the slices to the ice water. Drain again.

3. In a saucepan large enough to fit the orange slices in a single layer, combine the granulated sugar and 1 cup (240 ml) water over medium heat. Cook, stirring occasionally, until the sugar dissolves completely. Lower the heat to a simmer, add the orange slices in a single layer, and simmer on low, turning the orange slices every 15 minutes, until the skins turn translucent, about 1 hour. Using tongs, transfer the orange slices to a piece of parchment paper set on a wire rack and let cool overnight.

4. The next day, place the finely chopped chocolate in a microwave-safe bowl and heat in 30-second increments, stirring occasionally, until melted, or use the double-boiler method (see Note, page 44). Set aside to cool.

5. Dip the orange slices halfway in the melted chocolate and set onto a clean piece of parchment paper to dry.

linzer cookies

These jam-filled sandwich cookies make an appearance every year on my holiday table. Traditional Austrian linzer cookies are made using finely ground almonds in the dough, but I prefer the taste of finely ground toasted hazelnuts. Although linzers typically feature raspberry jam, feel free to use your favorites—I think apricot pairs especially nicely with the hazelnut biscuit. MAKES ABOUT 26 COOKIES, DEPENDING ON THE SIZE OF THE COOKIE CUTTERS

1 cup (135 g) whole hazelnuts, toasted

¾ cup (150 g) granulated sugar

2 cups (250 g) all-purpose flour

1 teaspoon (2 g) ground cinnamon

½ teaspoon (2.5 g) fine sea salt

1 cup (2 sticks/225 g) unsalted butter, room temperature

2 large egg yolks

1 teaspoon (5 ml) pure vanilla extract

½ cup (60 g) powdered sugar

⅓ cup plus 1 teaspoon (114 g) raspberry jam

⅓ cup plus 1 teaspoon (114 g) apricot jam

1. In a food processor, combine the hazelnuts and ¼ cup (50 g) of the granulated sugar and pulse until the hazelnuts are finely ground and the nuts and sugar are combined. Transfer to a medium bowl, then add the flour, cinnamon, and salt and whisk to combine.

2. In the bowl of a stand mixer fitted with the paddle attachment, beat the butter and the remaining ½ cup (100 g) granulated sugar together on medium-high until pale and fluffy, about 4 minutes. Add the egg yolks, one at a time, beating well after each addition. Add the vanilla and mix until combined. With the mixer on low, gradually add the flour mixture, mixing to combine.

3. Divide the dough in half, shape it into rounds, wrap in plastic wrap, and refrigerate at least 1 hour and preferably overnight.

4. Preheat the oven to 350°F (175°C). Line two baking trays with parchment paper or silicone baking mats.

5. Remove one piece of dough from the refrigerator and divide it in half. On a lightly floured work surface, roll each portion of dough out to about ¼ inch (5 mm) thickness. Use cookie cutters to cut out as many cookies as possible. Use a very small cookie cutter in the same shape to cut out the centers of half of the cookies—this is where the jam will be exposed once you sandwich them together.

6. Transfer the cookies to the prepared baking trays and refrigerate for 15 minutes, then bake for 10 to 12 minutes, or until lightly golden on top. Slide the parchment or silicone mats onto a wire rack and let the cookies cool completely. Repeat with the remaining dough.

7. When the cookies are completely cool, lightly dust the top cookies (with the cut-outs in the center) with powdered sugar. Spread a thin layer of raspberry or apricot jam on the bottom cookies, then top each one with a top cookie and gently press the two together.

iced sugar cookies

I wanted to include a classic iced sugar cookie in the bon voyage box, because they are Christmas in cookie form to me. The nostalgia and excitement of getting out your favorite cookie cutters and decorating just can't be beat. I like to use salted butter when making these, as I find it adds just a touch more flavor, but feel free to use unsalted—and a pinch of salt—if that's all you have on hand. As with most cookie doughs, the results are best when the dough has had time to chill, preferably overnight. It helps prevent spreading, which you definitely want to avoid when using cookie cutters with fine details like snowflakes. MAKES ABOUT 24 COOKIES, DEPENDING ON THE SIZE OF THE COOKIE CUTTERS

FOR THE COOKIES

¾ cup (1½ sticks/170 g) salted butter, room temperature

¾ cup (150 g) granulated sugar

1 large egg

½ teaspoon (2.5 ml) almond extract

1 large vanilla bean, split lengthwise *(see page 73 for vanilla bean note)*

2¼ cups (282 g) all-purpose flour

½ teaspoon (2 g) baking powder

FOR THE ROYAL ICING

½ cup (122 g) pasteurized egg whites (approximately 3 to 4 large egg whites)

4 cups (500 g) powdered sugar

1 teaspoon (5 ml) pure vanilla extract

Food coloring gel, such as Wilton (optional)

MAKE THE COOKIES

1. In the bowl of a stand mixer fitted with the paddle attachment, beat the butter and granulated sugar together on medium-high until pale and fluffy, about 4 minutes. Add the egg and almond extract. Using the tip of a sharp knife, scrape the seeds from the vanilla bean into the bowl and beat on high, scraping down the bowl as needed, until fully combined.

2. In a medium bowl, whisk together the flour and baking powder.

3. With the mixer on low, add the flour mixture in two additions, mixing well after each addition.

4. Divide the dough in half, flatten into rounds, cover with plastic wrap, and refrigerate overnight.

5. Preheat the oven to 350°F (175°C). Line two baking trays with parchment paper or silicone baking mats.

6. On a lightly floured work surface, roll out one portion of the dough to a roughly ¼ inch (5 mm) thickness. Use your favorite holiday cookie cutters to cut out shapes. Transfer the cookies to the prepared baking sheets then re-roll any scraps and cut out more cookies. Bake for 10 to 12 minutes for a softer texture and golden color or 12 to 15 minutes for a well-cooked texture and more browning around the edges. Slide the parchment or silicone mats onto a wire rack and let the cookies cool completely. Repeat with the remaining dough.

CONTINUED FROM PAGE 190

MAKE THE ROYAL ICING

1. In the bowl of a stand mixer fitted with the whisk attachment, beat the pasteurized egg whites on medium until soft peaks form. With the mixer on low, gradually add the powdered sugar in small batches, mixing well after each addition. When all the sugar has been added, add the vanilla and mix on high until stiff peaks form, about 5 minutes.

2. If coloring your icing, separate out as much icing as you would like to color—if you're using multiple colors, separate the icing into individual bowls. Gradually add color to your icing by dipping just the tip of a wooden toothpick into the food coloring gel and then swirling the color into the icing. Mix the icing to incorporate the color, gradually adding more food coloring gel until you get the shade you like.

3. Transfer each icing to a piping bag fitted with a very small round pastry tip. Have fun piping outlines and designs on the tops of the cookies and place on a wire rack. The royal icing will set within 4 to 6 hours.

chapter 5

les fêtes

{ celebrations }

EVERY SEASON IS a celebration of food in France. And nowhere does the French joy of good taste better culminate than with a fabulously festive fête, or party, Parisian-style. Whether it's a celebration of maman (mother) on Fête des Mères, a romantic champagne-fueled anniversaire (birthday), or the party to end all parties, Réveillon—when the most extravagant of French dishes are gathered on the table to be shared with close friends ringing in the New Year—the goal should always be clear: This is your moment to dial up the sparkle.

For me, this means a few things. Celebrating a big day is my cue to thumb through my most thoughtful recipes—the ones that take a little more effort or perhaps use a special ingredient. I might choose Sparkling Poire Belle Hélène (page 224), a simple-yet-glam dessert that features pears poached to perfection in champagne instead of traditional white wine. More often than not you'd catch me reaching for my Vanilla Celebration Cake recipe (page 200), a classic vanilla-on-vanilla confection that goes one luxurious step further than the rest, using two varieties of vanilla beans—Tahitian and Madagascan—one in the frosting, and one in the cake.

But sparkle doesn't have to stop at the recipe. Sometimes it's about how you embellish that dish with decoration. Take my Chocolate Truffles (page 211), for example. Simple and rich, some are dusted with cocoa powder, as you'd expect, but to create some drama, I've rolled others in gold sugar, a treat I picked up at La Grande Épicerie de Paris on rue de Sèvres (definitely grab some when next in town!). There's the decadent Crème Brûlée Cake (page 227), which I top with glass-like shards of burnt sugar to represent that satisfying act of cracking the caramelized layer of the creamy French classic with a spoon.

The last way I dial up a little wow-factor? Presentation and display. Though downright decadent on its own, Mousse au Chocolat (page 199) bubbles over with sophistication when served in vintage champagne coupes of varying sizes and designs. My modest Midnight Mendiants (page 223) make an elegant impression presented on a silver serving tray accompanied by a favorite champagne. And though I subscribe to the notion of using your good china every day, it's recipes like Chocolate and Raspberry Bombes (page 207), mini cakes lavishly coated in dark chocolate ganache and covered with a fresh pile of raspberries, that get the VIP treatment, being served on my very, *very* best dessert plates, beautiful gold-trimmed Christofle pieces that only come out when I'm in celebration mode.

When you're really ready for some revelry, however, you can dare to take it all on with the Ivoire Parisienne (page 212). The most challenging, over-the-top recipe in this chapter (and quite possibly the whole book), inspired by a beloved cake of mine from a well-known bakery in California, its multiple parts will take you some time. It's all worth it, though. After patiently baking its layers, filling them with white chocolate mousse and three types of berries, then wrapping it all in Italian meringue buttercream, you'll encrust it with white chocolate scrolls you'll curl by hand and top it with rose petals and edible gold leaf. The result is an "Oh, mon dieu!"–producing gasp from guests who'll know you went the extra mile to make your celebration one to remember. Sparkle absolutely guaranteed.

mousse au chocolat

I adore the simplicity of French chocolate mousse. Unlike its counterpart in the States, the French version is unsweetened and does not incorporate whipped cream, instead relying on only the whipped egg whites to give it its signature light and airy texture. It always elicits oohs and ahhs when brought out from the kitchen, especially when served in elegant champagne coupes. Plan to let the mousse set in the fridge for at least 4 hours, covering each glass with plastic wrap. Remove the glasses 30 minutes before serving to allow the mousse to come to room temperature. SERVES 6

7 ounces (200 g) 65% bittersweet chocolate, finely chopped

3 tablespoons (42 g) salted butter, room temperature

6 large eggs, separated

1 recipe Chantilly Cream (page 219)

2 ounces (56 g) 70% dark chocolate, freshly grated

1. Place the finely chopped chocolate and butter in a large heatproof bowl set over a pan of simmering water and stir until melted and smooth; set aside.

2. Place the egg whites in a small bowl and the egg yolks in the bowl of a stand mixer fitted with the whisk attachment. Whisk the egg yolks until rich and creamy like pudding, about 5 minutes. Add the egg yolk mixture to the melted chocolate and whisk until smooth.

3. In the clean bowl of a stand mixer fitted with the clean whisk attachment, whisk the egg whites until stiff peaks form. Using a rubber spatula, gently fold the egg whites into the chocolate mixture in three additions. Continue gently folding until the mousse is smooth and velvety.

4. Divide the mousse evenly among individual champagne coupes and refrigerate for at least 4 hours but preferably overnight.

5. Take the mousse out of the refrigerator about 30 minutes before serving. Top with Chantilly cream and sprinkle with freshly grated chocolate just before serving.

Note: Since this recipe uses raw eggs, I recommend consuming within 48 hours. You can also substitute pasteurized eggs.

vanilla celebration cake

Over the last few years, I've fielded the "favorite cake" question countless times, and the answer has never changed: classic vanilla cake with vanilla buttercream! And not just any buttercream, but, yes, classic *American* buttercream, the kind of buttercream you might find on sheet cakes in refrigerated cases of any grocery store in the US—sugary-sweet perfection. If there was a lavish cake buffet with every cake flavor imaginable, I would still reach for the humble and plain-to-some vanilla cake. When done right, it's sheer happiness on a plate (well, at least to me). I love baking with buttermilk, as it adds a pleasant tang to the cake and creates a softer crumb. In France, buttermilk is readily available at most supermarkets and is called lait ribot. I added two kinds of vanilla beans in this recipe—Tahitian, which imbues the cake with notes of cherry and spice, and Madagascan, which imparts a rich, buttery aroma to the frosting—but you can also use extract if that's what's in your pantry. Rainbow sprinkles are always an added bonus if you happen to have some on hand. SERVES 8 TO 10

MAKE THE VANILLA CAKE

1. Preheat the oven to 350°F (175°C). Grease and line three 6-inch (15-cm) round cake pans with parchment paper. Grease and flour the parchment paper. Set aside.

2. In a small bowl, combine the egg whites with the buttermilk. Using the tip of a sharp knife, scrape the vanilla bean seeds into the mixture and whisk to combine; set aside.

3. In the bowl of a stand mixer fitted with the paddle attachment, combine the cake flour, granulated sugar, and baking powder on low. With the mixer on low, gradually add the butter, 1 tablespoon (14 g) at a time, mixing well after each addition. Once all the butter has been added, slowly pour in half the egg white mixture, turn the speed up to medium, and mix until the batter is smooth. Turn the mixer back down to low and add the remaining egg white mixture. Mix until just combined. Using a rubber spatula, give the batter one more mix.

4. Divide the batter evenly among the prepared pans and bake for 30 to 35 minutes, or until a cake tester inserted into the centers comes out clean and the tops of the cakes are golden brown. Transfer the cakes to a wire rack to cool for 10 minutes before removing from the pans to cool completely.

FOR THE VANILLA CAKE

1 cup (2 sticks/225 g) salted butter, room temperature, plus additional for greasing

2¾ cups (305 g) cake flour, plus additional for dusting

5 large egg whites

1 cup (240 ml) buttermilk

1 Tahitian vanilla bean, split lengthwise (see page 73)

1½ cups (300 g) granulated sugar

1 tablespoon (12 g) baking powder

FOR THE VANILLA BUTTERCREAM

¼ cup (60 ml) heavy cream, plus additional as needed

1 Madagascan vanilla bean, split lengthwise *(see page 73 for vanilla bean note)*

2 cups (4 sticks/450 g) unsalted butter, room temperature

4⅔ cups (584 g) powdered sugar

Pinch of fleur de sel or coarse sea salt

FOR THE ASSEMBLY

Rainbow sprinkles (optional)

CONTINUED FROM PAGE 200

MAKE THE VANILLA BUTTERCREAM

1. Meanwhile, place the heavy cream in a small bowl. Using the tip of a sharp knife, scrape the vanilla bean seeds into the cream. Whisk to combine and set aside.

2. In the bowl of a stand mixer fitted with the paddle attachment, beat the butter on medium-high until pale, 4 to 5 minutes. With the mixer on low, gradually add the powdered sugar, ½ cup (60 g) at a time, mixing well after each addition. Add the vanilla-infused cream and the salt and beat on medium-high until smooth and fluffy, 2 to 3 minutes. If you prefer a fluffier buttercream, gradually add splashes of heavy cream until the frosting is smooth and spreadable.

ASSEMBLY

1. Using a serrated knife, level the cakes by trimming off the tops. Spread a small spoonful of buttercream onto the center of a cake plate or stand to secure the cake, and place the first cake layer directly on top. Divide the total buttercream roughly in half and set aside one portion for covering and decorating.

2. Using an offset palette knife, spread an even layer of buttercream on top of the first cake layer and place the next cake layer on top. Spread an even layer of buttercream on top and finish with the last cake layer. Using what is left of the first portion of buttercream, spread a thin layer over the sides and top of the cake, then transfer to the refrigerator to allow the crumb coat to set, about 20 minutes.

3. Cover the sides and top of the cake with an even layer of the reserved buttercream. Transfer any remaining buttercream to a piping bag fitted with a medium French star pastry tip and decorate the cake with dollops, rosettes, or pearls. Finish with the rainbow sprinkles, if using.

tarragon and comté sablés

Putting together the perfect cheese platter is truly an art form the French have perfected. Though I've not yet tried all the various cheeses in France (at last count, they numbered over 1,600!), I've certainly found my favorites, including summer Beaufort, in which you find notes of the wildflowers and grasses the cows graze on in summertime; Saint-Marcellin, whose creaminess and mushroomlike flavor is best enjoyed warmed lightly in the oven; and a stunning dried flower–encrusted round of cheese called Belval. At almost every apéro, or happy hour, I've been invited to, there have been animated discussions about which cheese is a must-try and which ones to avoid. Along with every cheese board (see page 204), there are a few salty condiments mixed in, such as olives or cornichons, a sweet element like quince paste or fig jam, and, of course, heaps of bread or savory crackers to serve as vehicles for all that mouthwatering cheese. For this sablé, or shortbread, recipe, I chose tarragon, which French chefs often refer to as the "King of Herbs," for its peppery notes, which contrast nicely with the fruity quality of Comté cheese, a hard Alpine cheese. These crackers can also stand on their own with a glass of champagne served at your next apéro! MAKES 24 SABLÉS

6 ounces (170 g) Comté cheese, grated

8 tablespoons (1 stick/113 g) unsalted butter, softened

1½ tablespoons (5 g) finely chopped fresh tarragon leaves or 1 heaped teaspoon (1 g) dried tarragon

2 teaspoons (4 g) coarsely ground black pepper

½ teaspoon (2.5 g) fine sea salt

1⅓ cups (167 g) all-purpose flour, plus more for dusting

1. In the bowl of a stand mixer fitted with the paddle attachment, beat the grated cheese, butter, tarragon, pepper, and salt on medium until combined, about 2 minutes. With the mixer on low, gradually add the flour, mixing until fully combined. Transfer the dough to a lightly floured work surface and use your hands to shape it into a log, 6 to 7 inches (15 to 18 cm) long. Wrap tightly in plastic wrap and refrigerate for at least 1 hour but preferably overnight.

2. Preheat the oven to 350°F (175°C). Line two baking trays with parchment paper or silicone baking mats; set aside.

3. Remove the dough from the refrigerator and allow to rest for a few minutes at room temperature. Using a sharp knife, cut the log into rounds ¼ inch (5 mm) thick and place on the prepared baking trays. Bake for 15 to 20 minutes, or until golden on top. Slide the parchment paper or silicone mats onto wire racks and let the sablés cool completely. (Sablés will keep in an airtight container at room temperature for up to 5 days.)

cheese, please

Here's my formula for creating a cheese board à la française.

KNOW YOUR NUMBERS. An odd number of cheeses works best and also happens to look lovely when arranged together. In terms of how much to buy, my rule of thumb is 1 to 2 ounces (28 to 57 g) of each cheese for every guest.

AIM FOR VARIETY. French cheeses are from the milk of cows, goats, and sheep, so offer a mix. You'll want a range of flavors (mild, tangy, aged, blue, and yes, stinky) and textures (hard, soft, crumbly). I also look for different shapes, such as pyramids, squares, and rounds, as well as cheeses with interesting coatings, like dried flowers, herbs, or crushed pepper.

GET SWEET & SALTY. The natural sweetness of fruit (like grapes, figs, kumquats, or dried apricots), fig jam, quince paste, and honey can accompany cheese beautifully and give color to your spread. The same thinking goes with salty items—nuts, olives, cornichons, and the like—which add balance and choice.

BRING ON THE BREAD. It's another rule in France: Most of the time, you simply cannot serve cheese without bread. Baguette, of course, always works, as does a more rustic "country" bread or a sourdough. I also like to serve a selection of savory crackers such as my Tarragon and Comté Sablés (page 203).

PRESENT WITH PANACHE. Arrange everything artfully—as with most French creations, you want to please the eye before you please the stomach! For a foundation, a slate or wooden board are classics, but I also like to experiment with vintage trays and plates for a touch of personality. And don't forget cheese knives; I like a set that can tackle both hard or soft servings with aplomb.

chocolate and raspberry bombes

I think we all can agree that chocolate and raspberry is a match made in food-pairing heaven. Though small in size, these mini bombes deliver a decadent explosion of flavor in each forkful. With a rich chocolate cake filled with raspberry jam and coated twice in luxurious chocolate ganache, these are the elegant answer to your dinner-party dessert question. And the best part? They can be prepared the night before and somehow taste even better after all that ganache has had time to chill and set. SERVES 6

MAKE THE CAKES

1. Preheat the oven to 350°F (175°C). Grease and line six 4-inch (10-cm) round cake pans with parchment paper. Grease and flour the parchment paper. Set aside.

2. In a large bowl, whisk together the flour, granulated sugar, sifted cocoa powder, baking powder, baking soda, and salt. Pour the hot coffee in a slow stream into the flour mixture while whisking. Add the buttermilk and whisk until incorporated. Add the oil and whisk until fully incorporated. Add the eggs, one at a time, mixing well after each addition. Add the vanilla and give the batter one last stir.

3. Divide the batter evenly among the prepared pans and bake for 30 to 35 minutes, or until a cake tester inserted into the centers comes out clean— the cakes will rise and crack on top. Transfer the cakes to a wire rack to cool for 15 minutes before removing from the pans to cool completely.

MAKE THE GANACHE

1. Meanwhile, place the finely chopped bittersweet chocolate in a medium heatproof bowl.

2. In a small saucepan set over medium heat, bring the heavy cream just to a boil. Pour the hot cream over the chocolate and let stand for 2 minutes, then stir until the chocolate is smooth and melted. Keep warm.

ASSEMBLY

1. Using a serrated knife, level the cakes by trimming off the tops.

2. Using a cupcake corer or a tablespoon, scoop a small cavity out of the top center of each cake, reserving the scooped-out pieces of cake. Fill each cavity with 2 tablespoons (40 g) seedless raspberry jam. Use the reserved cake pieces to cover the cavities and give the cakes smooth tops.

FOR THE CAKES

Unsalted butter, for greasing

2½ cups (315 g) all-purpose flour, plus additional for dusting

2 cups (400 g) granulated sugar

½ cup (50 g) Dutch-process cocoa powder, sifted

2 teaspoons (8 g) baking powder

2 teaspoons (8 g) baking soda

½ teaspoon (2.5 g) fine sea salt

1 cup (240 ml) strongly brewed coffee, hot

1 cup (240 ml) buttermilk

½ cup (120 ml) sunflower oil

2 large eggs, room temperature

1½ teaspoons (7.5 ml) pure vanilla extract

FOR THE GANACHE

9 ounces (252 g) 65% bittersweet chocolate, finely chopped

1 cup plus 2 tablespoons (270 ml) heavy cream

FOR THE ASSEMBLY

¾ cup (240 g) seedless raspberry jam

12 ounces (336 g) raspberries, for serving

Powdered sugar, for dusting (optional)

CONTINUED FROM PAGE 207

3. Set the cakes on a wire rack placed over a piece of parchment paper. Set aside about ⅔ of the ganache, then use the rest to pour a thin layer over the top and sides of the cakes—think of this as the crumb coat. Transfer the cakes to the refrigerator to set for 40 minutes. Leave the ganache at room temperature.

4. Remove the cakes from the refrigerator and place on individual dessert plates. Using an offset palette knife, spread the reserved ganache—it will have thickened to a frosting-like consistency—over the sides and tops of the cakes. Arrange raspberries on top of each cake. Place the cakes in the refrigerator to set, at least 1 hour. Finish with a light dusting of powdered sugar right before serving, if desired.

chocolate truffles

There's no easier way to prepare an elegant and irresistible treat for any fête than with these divine chocolate truffles. Since their main ingredient is chocolate, I encourage you to use the highest quality you can find. Single-origin would be ideal, plus it makes for interesting party chatter as you offer guests a taste of Brazil or Venezuela via your homemade truffles. I like to roll some of these in traditional cocoa powder, and then some in gold sugar for that extra sparkle. MAKES 20 TO 24 TRUFFLES

8 ounces (225 g) 65% bittersweet chocolate, finely chopped

⅔ cup (160 ml) heavy cream

½ teaspoon (7.5 ml) pure vanilla extract

Dutch-process cocoa powder, for coating

Gold sugar, for coating (optional)

1. Place the finely chopped bittersweet chocolate in a medium heatproof bowl.

2. In a small saucepan set over medium heat, bring the heavy cream to a gentle boil. Pour the cream over the chocolate and let sit for 2 minutes before whisking in the vanilla. Mix until smooth and shiny. Transfer to the refrigerator to set, 1 to 2 hours.

3. Working quickly, use a tablespoon to scoop the ganache into heaping tablespoon portions, then use your hands to roll them into smooth balls. Coat the truffles by rolling in cocoa powder, gold sugar, or the topping of your choice. Truffles taste best at room temperature. (Truffles will keep in an airtight container at room temperature for up to 5 days.)

ivoire parisienne

This cake was my obsession when I lived in California. I even remember my better half picking up a slice in my hometown of San Diego and hand-carrying it on a flight to San Francisco to surprise me at university (now that's love!). The original cake, named "Ivoire Royale," is a confection featuring white chocolate, berries, vanilla-soaked sponge cake, and whipped cream, and is the brainchild of Paris-trained pastry chef Karen Krasne, who also happens to own San Diego's most magical cake shop, Extraordinary Desserts. In this version, I've stuck closely to her recipe, just substituting Italian meringue frosting for the whipped cream original, mostly because I find whipped cream frosting tricky to work with. And yes, there are multiple components to creating this cake and, yes, curling all that white chocolate can be time consuming (and the mousse should set overnight). But I assure you it all comes together to create a romantic rose petal, berry, and white chocolate–laden, gold-leaf extravaganza that's perfect for an over-the-top fête like Réveillon . . . or any other celebration where you'd like to truly impress your guests. You'll have leftover white chocolate mousse from this recipe, which can be paired with berries or dark chocolate shavings for individual parfaits. SERVES 12 TO 14

FOR THE WHITE CHOCOLATE CURLS

8 ounces (225 g) white chocolate, finely chopped

2 teaspoons (9 g) unsalted butter

FOR THE WHITE CHOCOLATE MOUSSE

6½ ounces (182 g) white chocolate, finely chopped

1¼ cups (300 ml) heavy cream

8½ ounces (238 g) crème fraîche, room temperature

FOR THE CAKE

1½ cups (3 sticks/336 g) unsalted butter, room temperature, plus additional for greasing

4 cups (500 g) all-purpose flour, plus additional for dusting

3¼ teaspoons (13 g) baking powder

½ teaspoon (2.5 g) fine sea salt

1½ cups plus 1 tablespoon (375 ml) whole milk

4½ ounces (126 g) crème fraîche

2 teaspoons (10 ml) pure vanilla extract

2 cups (400 g) granulated sugar

4 large eggs, room temperature

2 large egg whites, room temperature

MAKE THE WHITE CHOCOLATE CURLS

1. In a microwave-safe bowl, combine the finely chopped white chocolate and butter. Microwave in 30-second increments, stirring occasionally, until melted, or use the double-boiler method (see Note, page 44). Pour the melted chocolate on the backs of two clean baking trays and use an offset palette knife to spread it into a thin, even layer that covers most of the tray. Transfer the baking trays to the refrigerator and allow the chocolate to set, 30 to 45 minutes.

2. Carefully and slowly drag a bench scraper or metal spatula from one end of the chocolate to the other to create curls. If the chocolate softens, return the pan to the refrigerator for 5 to 10 minutes. You can make various sizes of curls to add more interest and texture to the cake. Transfer the chocolate curls to a plate and refrigerate until ready to use.

MAKE THE WHITE CHOCOLATE MOUSSE

1. Place the finely chopped white chocolate in a medium heatproof bowl.

2. In a small saucepan set over medium-high heat, bring the heavy cream to a gentle boil. Once the cream is gently boiling, pour over the chocolate and let it sit for a couple minutes before whisking until smooth.

CONTINUED FROM PAGE 212

Add the crème fraîche in two additions, whisking until smooth and fully combined. Cover with plastic wrap, pressing it directly on the surface of the mousse to prevent a skin forming, and refrigerate to set overnight.

MAKE THE CAKE

1. Preheat the oven to 350°F (175°C). Grease and line three 8-inch (20-cm) cake rounds with parchment paper. Grease and flour the parchment paper. Set aside.

2. In a medium bowl, whisk together the flour, baking powder, and salt; set aside.

3. In a small bowl, whisk together the milk, crème fraîche, and vanilla; set aside.

4. In the bowl of a stand mixer fitted with the paddle attachment, beat the butter and granulated sugar together until pale and fluffy, about 4 minutes. With the mixer on low, add the whole eggs, one at a time, followed by the 2 egg whites, scraping down the bowl with a rubber spatula between additions. Add the flour mixture in 3 additions, alternating with the milk mixture, and mix until just combined. Be careful not to overmix.

5. Divide the batter evenly among the prepared pans and bake for 35 to 40 minutes, or until a cake tester inserted into the centers comes out clean and the cakes are golden brown. Transfer the cakes to a wire rack to cool for 10 minutes before removing from the pans to cool completely.

MAKE THE VANILLA SIMPLE SYRUP

1. Combine the granulated sugar with ½ cup (120 ml) water in a small saucepan over medium-high heat and bring to a boil. Once the sugar has dissolved completely, remove from the heat, transfer to a heatproof bowl, and let cool completely.

2. Once the syrup is completely cool, stir in the vanilla and 2 tablespoons (30 ml) water. (The vanilla syrup will keep in an airtight container in the refrigerator for up to 3 days.)

MAKE THE ITALIAN MERINGUE BUTTERCREAM

1. Combine the granulated sugar and ¼ cup (60 ml) water in a small saucepan set over high heat. Bring to a boil and continue cooking until the syrup reaches soft-ball stage, or 240°F (115°C) on a candy thermometer, 8 to 10 minutes.

FOR THE VANILLA SIMPLE SYRUP

½ cup (100 g) granulated sugar

2 tablespoons (30 ml) pure vanilla extract

FOR THE ITALIAN MERINGUE BUTTERCREAM

1 cup (200 g) granulated sugar

4 large egg whites

⅛ teaspoon (.5 g) fine sea salt

2 cups (4 sticks/450 g) unsalted butter, room temperature

2 teaspoons (10 ml) pure vanilla extract

FOR THE ASSEMBLY

1 cup (5 ounces/140 g) blackberries

1 cup (5 ounces/140 g) blueberries

1¼ cups (5 ounces/140 g) raspberries

8 rose petals

Edible gold leaf (optional); see page 216

2. Meanwhile, in the bowl of a stand mixer fitted with the whisk attachment, whisk the egg whites and salt on high until stiff peaks form.

3. Once the syrup has reached 240°F (115°C), carefully pour it into the egg white mixture in a slow steady stream with the mixer on low. Once all the syrup has been added, turn the mixer up to high and whisk until cool, about 5 minutes.

4. With the mixer set to medium-high, add the butter, 1 tablespoon (14 g) at a time, until fully combined. Once all the butter has been added, add the vanilla and whip on high until light and fluffy, 4 to 5 minutes more.

ASSEMBLY

1. Using a serrated knife, level the cakes by trimming off the tops. Brush the vanilla simple syrup on the cut sides of all the cake layers. Spread a small spoonful of buttercream onto the center of a cake plate or stand to secure the cake, and place the first cake layer directly on top. Transfer about a third of the buttercream to a piping bag fitted with a medium French star pastry tip and set aside for decorating.

2. Transfer another third of the buttercream to a piping bag fitted with a medium round pastry tip and pipe a circle of buttercream on the top outer edge of the cake. Fill the circle with about a quarter of the white chocolate mousse. Sprinkle the blackberries and blueberries over the mousse, staying inside the piped circle of frosting. Top with the second cake layer and repeat the process with the frosting and mousse, but this time, use the raspberries. (Reserve remaining mousse for another use.) Place the final cake layer on top. Use some of the remaining buttercream to spread a thin layer of frosting over the sides and top of the cake, then transfer to the refrigerator to allow the crumb coat to set, about 20 minutes.

3. Cover the sides and top of the cake in an even layer with the remaining buttercream and use your offset palette knife to smooth out the top and sides.

4. Cover the sides of the cake with the white chocolate curls. Using the buttercream in the piping bag fitted with the medium French star pastry tip, pipe a border around the top outer edge of the cake. Place rose petals on top of the piped border and fill the center of the cake with more white chocolate curls. Lightly brush some of the rose petals with edible gold leaf for a glamorous finish, if using. Keep refrigerated until ready to serve.

decorating with edible gold leaf

Use edible gold leaf to adorn your desserts with a touch of golden glamour. I like to use loose-leaf sheets that are sold in tiny envelopes, perfect for garnishing cakes, fruit, meringue, and chocolate. Working with edible gold leaf can be tricky, since it's such a delicate product, but with practice, you'll soon find yourself wanting to give everything the golden treatment.

Use a precision knife to cut a partial piece of the gold leaf. Lightly dampen the surface of whatever it is you will be decorating with water and carefully pick up the piece of gold leaf using the precision knife and a small paintbrush. Next, use the paintbrush to smooth it down onto your surface.

If you'd like to cover a whole cake in gold, I recommend using transfer gold leaf instead. I've seen various shades from rose gold to champagne-toned. It has a very long shelf life if stored in a cool, dry place.

mont-blanc mess

Le Mont-Blanc, a dome of meringue covered in both whipped cream and chestnut paste, is one of my all-time favorite French pastries, mainly because I'm obsessed with crème de marron—a puree of chestnuts mixed with sugar and vanilla and sold in tins in most grocery stores in France. When I first moved to Paris, it was a hard sell for me, as I simply had never been acquainted with this questionable-looking brown paste. However, once I tried it with a dollop of airy whipped cream and a crunchy meringue, I never looked back. This recipe was inspired in part by the delicious simplicity of an English Eton mess—strawberries, meringue, and whipped cream, usually served together in a glass—but with the flavors of a classic Mont-Blanc. This recipe is a no-fuss dessert that's easy to assemble before your guests arrive for any type of soirée. SERVES 6

MAKE THE MERINGUES

1. Preheat the oven to 225°F (105°C). Line a baking tray with parchment paper or a silicone baking mat; set aside.

2. In the bowl of a stand mixer fitted with the whisk attachment, add the egg whites, vanilla, and salt. Whisk the egg whites beginning on low and gradually moving to high until stiff peaks form. With the mixer on high, slowly add the granulated sugar, 1 tablespoon (12.5 g) at a time, and mix well after each addition. Once all the sugar has been added, continue mixing on high until smooth and stiff, about 5 minutes more. Transfer to a piping bag and cut off the end so the opening is roughly the size of a quarter. Holding the piping bag vertically and directly above the prepared baking tray, squeeze out a large dollop of meringue (approximately the size of a golf ball) and pull up to create a large kiss shape with a pointed tip. Repeat with the remaining meringue. Bake for 45 to 60 minutes, or until the parchment paper easily peels off the meringues. Turn off the oven and leave the meringues to dry out in the oven for several hours or overnight.

MAKE THE CHANTILLY CREAM

1. Place the stand mixer bowl and whisk attachment in the refrigerator to chill for 20 minutes before using.

2. Pour the heavy cream into the chilled stand mixer bowl. Using the tip of a sharp knife, scrape the seeds from the vanilla bean into the bowl. Add the powdered sugar and use the chilled whisk attachment to whip on high until stiff peaks form, 3 to 5 minutes. Cover and refrigerate until ready to use.

FOR THE MERINGUES

5½ ounces (154 g) egg whites (about 4 large egg whites)

1 teaspoon (5 ml) pure vanilla extract

Pinch of fine sea salt

1½ cups (300 g) granulated sugar

(See pavlova recipe for precise measurements, page 98)

FOR THE CHANTILLY CREAM

1¼ cups (300 ml) heavy cream, cold

1 vanilla bean, split lengthwise *(see page 73 for vanilla bean note)*

¾ cup (90 g) powdered sugar

FOR THE ASSEMBLY

18 ounces (510 g) crème de marrons (chestnut cream)

Powdered sugar, for dusting

CONTINUED FROM PAGE 219

ASSEMBLY

1. Line up six champagne coupes or glass ice cream dishes and divide the crème de marron evenly among the glasses.

2. Set aside six of the meringues. Roughly crush the rest of the meringues and sprinkle over the chestnut cream.

3. Transfer the Chantilly cream to a piping bag fitted with a medium open star pastry tip, and pipe a mound of Chantilly cream over the crushed meringue layer. Place a whole meringue on top of the Chantilly cream in each dish, then dust each coupe with powdered sugar to resemble fallen snow.

midnight mendiants

Mendiants are a classic French Christmas confection that have been around since the Middle Ages. The small chocolate discs were originally topped with dried fruits and nuts to symbolize the four Roman Catholic mendicant monastic orders of the day: dried figs (purple) represented the Augustinians; almonds (white), the Dominicans; raisins (gray) were for the Franciscans; and hazelnuts (brown) signified the Carmelites. Today the toppings have somewhat diversified, as I've spotted dried goji berries, slivers of candied pink grapefruit, and cashew nuts in some of the more modern chocolatiers of Paris. Choosing your favorite toppings is part of the fun in making these mendiants—just be sure to use a high-quality bittersweet chocolate (Bonnat or Valrhona are both excellent French chocolate choices) since it's the real star of this show. I like to put out a tray of these for special celebrations, as they make a sweet pairing with a glass of champagne. MAKES 15 TO 20 MENDIANTS

6 ounces (170 g) 70% dark chocolate, finely chopped

½ cup (86 g) chopped dried apricots

½ cup (75 g) chopped dried figs

¼ cup (40 g) chopped pistachios

¼ cup (29 g) chopped roasted hazelnuts

¼ cup (35 g) chopped dried cranberries

1. Place the finely chopped dark chocolate in a microwave-safe bowl and heat in 30-second increments, stirring occasionally, until melted, or use the double-boiler method (see Note, page 44). Set aside to cool.

2. Line two baking trays with parchment paper or silicone baking mats. Drop tablespoon-sized dollops of chocolate on the prepared trays, at least 2 inches (5 cm) apart. Bang the trays on the counter once to spread the chocolate a bit.

3. Place pieces of the apricots, figs, pistachios, hazelnuts, and cranberries on top of each chocolate disc—work quickly while the chocolate is still liquid. Transfer the trays to the refrigerator to allow the mendiants to set, 20 to 30 minutes. (Mendiants can be stored in an airtight container at room temperature for up to 5 days.)

sparkling poire belle hélène

Legendary French pastry chef Auguste Escoffier first concocted this classic dessert during La Belle Époque ("the Beautiful Epoch") of nineteenth-century Paris. Named after *La Belle Hélène*, or *The Beautiful Helen* by Jacques Offenbach, this traditional recipe calls for poaching the pears in either white wine or a spice syrup, but I've chosen to up the glam factor a tiny bit by poaching them in champagne . . . D'Anjou pears would make a fine substitute if you can't find Conference at your local market. SERVES 4

MAKE THE POACHED PEARS

1. Peel the pears and slice a sliver off the bottom of each, as this will allow them to sit upright when you plate them after poaching.

2. In a medium saucepan, combine the champagne, granulated sugar, cinnamon stick, and star anise pod. Using the tip of a sharp knife, scrape the seeds from the vanilla bean into the pan. Add the scraped vanilla bean as well and bring the mixture to a boil, then reduce the heat to low and gently add the pears. Simmer the pears, occasionally spooning some of the liquid over the pears, for 15 minutes, or until the pears are tender—you can test them with a small knife. Carefully transfer the pears to individual plates.

MAKE THE CHANTILLY CREAM

1. Place the stand mixer bowl and whisk attachment in the refrigerator to chill for 20 minutes before using.

2. Pour the cold heavy cream into the chilled stand mixer bowl. Using the tip of a sharp knife, scrape the seeds from the vanilla bean into the bowl. Add the powdered sugar and use the chilled whisk attachment to whip on high until stiff peaks form, 3 to 5 minutes. Cover and refrigerate until ready to use.

MAKE THE CHOCOLATE SAUCE

1. Meanwhile, in a small saucepan over medium heat, combine the butter and heavy cream and bring to a simmer, stirring until the butter has melted completely.

2. Turn off the heat and stir in the chopped dark chocolate and vanilla. Keep warm.

ASSEMBLY

Pour the warm chocolate sauce over the top of each pear, then add a dollop of Chantilly cream. If using, add cinnamon sticks and a star anise pod next to each pear. To add a little festive glamour, brush edible gold leaf onto the stems of each pear.

FOR THE POACHED PEARS

4 pears, ideally Conference pears

1 (750-ml) bottle champagne

1 cup (200 g) granulated sugar

1 cinnamon stick

1 star anise pod

1 vanilla bean, split lengthwise

FOR THE CHANTILLY CREAM

1 cup plus 2 tablespoons (270 ml) heavy cream, cold

1 vanilla bean, split lengthwise (see page 73)

3½ tablespoons (27 g) powdered sugar

FOR THE CHOCOLATE SAUCE

2 tablespoons (28 g) salted butter

⅔ cup (160 ml) heavy cream

6 ounces (170 g) 70% dark chocolate, finely chopped

½ teaspoon (2.5 ml) pure vanilla extract

FOR THE ASSEMBLY (OPTIONAL)

8 cinnamon sticks

4 star anise pods

Edible gold leaf (see page 216)

crème brûlée cake

I don't think I've ever met anyone who doesn't love crème brûlée, a rich custard topped with a layer of hardened caramelized sugar. One of the joys of eating this treat is, of course, tapping your spoon on top to hear the unmistakable sound of burnt sugar breaking to reveal the cream below. This cake version features layers of yellow cake filled with rich vanilla bean pastry cream meant to evoke the flavor of crème brûlée, plus a beurre noisette, or burnt butter, frosting. The decorative sugar glass is beautiful and just as satisfying to break as the top of traditional crème brûlée—feel free to serve extra broken shards with every slice. This is one of my go-to birthday cake recipes, but it would also make an ideal party cake. SERVES 12

MAKE THE VANILLA BEAN PASTRY CREAM

1. Place the heavy cream in a medium saucepan set over medium-high heat. Using the tip of a sharp knife, scrape the seeds from the vanilla bean into the pan. Bring to a gentle boil.

2. In a medium bowl, whisk together the egg yolks, granulated sugar, cornstarch, and salt until thick and smooth. Once the cream has reached a gentle boil, pour half of it into the egg yolk mixture, whisking continuously. Once the egg mixture has been tempered, add it back to the saucepan with the remaining hot cream, whisking continuously. Return to the heat and continue to whisk the entire mixture until it begins to thicken, about 2 minutes. Once it thickens, lower the heat and continue to cook, stirring, for an additional 2 to 3 minutes.

3. Turn off the heat and add the butter, 1 tablespoon (14 g) at a time, whisking until smooth and velvety. Transfer the pastry cream to a bowl and cover with plastic wrap, pressing it on the surface of the cream to prevent a skin forming. Allow to cool for 30 minutes at room temperature before transferring to the refrigerator to set, at least 3 hours or overnight.

MAKE THE CAKE

1. Preheat the oven to 350°F (175°C). Grease and line three 6-inch (15-cm) round cake pans with parchment paper. Grease and flour the parchment paper. Set aside.

2. In a medium bowl, whisk together the whole eggs, egg yolks, milk, yogurt, and vanilla until combined; set aside.

FOR THE VANILLA BEAN
PASTRY CREAM

2 cups (480 ml) heavy cream

1 vanilla bean, split lengthwise
(see page 73 for vanilla bean note)

5 large egg yolks, room temperature

6 tablespoons (75 g) granulated sugar

¼ cup (32 g) cornstarch

Pinch of fine sea salt

¼ cup (½ stick/56 g) unsalted butter

FOR THE CAKE

1 cup (2 sticks/225 g) unsalted butter, room temperature, plus additional for greasing

2¼ cups (252 g) cake flour, plus additional for dusting

2 large eggs, room temperature

2 large egg yolks, room temperature

¾ cup (180 ml) whole milk

¼ cup (60 g) plain whole-milk Greek yogurt

1 teaspoon (5 ml) pure vanilla extract

1½ cups (300 g) granulated sugar

1 tablespoon (12 g) baking powder

¼ teaspoon (1 g) baking soda

½ teaspoon (2.5 g) fine sea salt

CONTINUED FROM PAGE 227

3. In the bowl of a stand mixer fitted with the paddle attachment, combine the cake flour, granulated sugar, baking powder, baking soda, and salt. With the mixer on low, add the butter, 1 tablespoon (14 g) at a time. Once all the butter has been added, turn the mixer up to medium and beat until the mixture resembles coarse sand. With the mixer on low, slowly add half of the milk mixture and mix until incorporated. Add the second half of the milk mixture, turn the mixer up to medium, and mix until just combined.

4. Divide the batter evenly among the prepared pans and bake 30 to 35 minutes, or until a cake tester inserted into the centers comes out clean and the cakes are golden brown. Transfer the cakes to a wire rack to cool for 15 minutes before removing from the pans to cool completely.

MAKE THE BEURRE NOISETTE FROSTING

1. In a medium saucepan set over medium heat, melt the butter and cook until fragrant and amber brown, 8 to 10 minutes. Transfer immediately to a small heatproof bowl and let cool at room temperature for 15 minutes. Cover with plastic wrap and transfer to the refrigerator to chill until firm, about 1 hour, stirring periodically to prevent separation.

2. Remove the butter from the refrigerator and let stand at room temperature for a few minutes, then place in the bowl of a stand mixer fitted with the paddle attachment, and beat on high until fluffy, 4 to 5 minutes. Reduce the speed to low and gradually add the powdered sugar, 1 cup (125 g) at a time, scraping down the bowl with a rubber spatula between additions. Add the heavy cream and vanilla and beat on high until smooth, 4 to 5 minutes.

MAKE THE SUGAR SHARDS

1. Prepare two pieces of parchment paper, each about the size of a baking tray. Place one on a kitchen counter or other heatproof surface and set the other piece aside. Pour the sugar into a large heavy-bottomed pan and set over medium heat. Do not stir. Once the sugar dissolves, turn the heat up to medium-high and cook, without stirring, until the sugar is dark amber—keep a close eye on it.

2. Carefully pour the hot sugar directly in the center of the prepared parchment paper and immediately place the second piece of parchment paper directly on top. Being careful not to touch the hot mixture with your hands, use a rolling pin to carefully roll the sugar out flat before it sets. Allow to cool and harden, 5 to 10 minutes.

FOR THE BEURRE NOISETTE FROSTING

2 cups (4 sticks/450 g) unsalted butter, room temperature

5 cups (625 g) powdered sugar

1 tablespoon (15 ml) heavy cream

1 teaspoon (5 ml) pure vanilla extract

FOR THE SUGAR SHARDS

¾ cup (150 g) granulated sugar

3. Once the sugar has set, peel the top piece of parchment paper off and break apart the sugar into various-sized shards. If not using immediately, store the sugar shards in a resealable plastic bag in the freezer until ready to use.

ASSEMBLY

1. Using a serrated knife, level the cakes by trimming off the tops. Spread a small spoonful of frosting onto the center of a cake plate or stand to secure the cake, and place the first cake layer directly on top. Transfer about a third of the frosting to a piping bag fitted with a medium round pastry tip and pipe a circle of frosting around the top outer edge of the cake round. Fill the circle with about ¼ cup (60 ml) of the vanilla bean pastry cream. Place the next cake layer on top and repeat the process (there will be leftover pastry cream). Place the last cake layer on top.

2. Use some of the remaining frosting to spread a thin layer of frosting over the sides and top of the cake with an offset palette knife, then transfer to the refrigerator to allow the crumb coat to set, about 20 minutes.

3. Cover the sides and top of the cake in an even layer with the remaining frosting. Decorate the cake by pushing shards of sugar into the top, using various sizes to create some dimension and drama in your design. Keep refrigerated until ready to serve.

paris addresses

Get to know the city throughout the seasons with some of the spots mentioned in the book
(as well as a few additional favorites).

coffee

Any of these spots will whip you up the perfect cuppa!

BACK IN BLACK
25 Rue Amelot, 75011 Paris
backinblackcoffee.com

BOOT CAFÉ
19 Rue du Pont aux Choux,
75003 Paris
01 73 70 14 57
Instagram: bootcafe

CAFÉ KITSUNÉ PALAIS ROYAL
51 Galerie de Montpensier,
75001 Paris
01 40 15 62 31
maisonkitsune.com

COUTUME BABYLONE
47 Rue de Babylone, 75007 Paris
09 88 40 47 99
coutumecafe.com

DREAMIN' MAN
140 Rue Amelot, 75011 Paris
Instagram: dreaminman_paris

HOLYBELLY
5 Rue Lucien Sampaix, 75010 Paris
01 82 28 00 80
holybellycafe.com

KB CAFÉSHOP
53 Avenue Trudaine, 75009 Paris
01 56 92 12 41
kbcoffeeroasters.com

LOUSTIC CAFÉ
40 Rue Chapon, 75003 Paris
09 80 31 07 06
cafeloustic.com

PARTISAN CAFÉ ARTISANAL
36 Rue de Turbigo, 75003 Paris
parispartisancafe.com

TEN BELLES
10 Rue de la Grange aux Belles,
75010 Paris
09 83 08 86 69
tenbelles.com

TÉLESCOPE CAFÉ
5 Rue Villédo, 75001 Paris
Instagram: telescopecafe

THE DANCING GOAT
117 Avenue Gambetta, 75020 Paris
Instagram: thedancinggoatparis

CHANCEUX
57 Rue Saint-Maur, 75011 Paris
Instagram: chanceux.paris

chocolate

LE CHOCOLAT ALAIN DUCASSE
Try the coconut praliné and his sophisticated single-origin ganache chocolates!
26 Rue Saint-Benoît, 75006 Paris
01 45 48 87 89

Factory address where the roasting happens: 40 Rue de la Roquette, 75011 Paris

lechocolat-alainducasse.com/en

PATRICK ROGER
A sleek and avant-garde chocolate house in a beautiful spot; special mention to his lime and basil chocolate.
2-4 Place Saint-Sulpice, 75006 Paris
01 43 29 88 25
patrickroger.com

DEBAUVE & GALLAIS
One of Paris's oldest chocolate shops, where you can try "Pistoles de Marie-Antoinette," chocolate medallions created especially for the queen herself.
30 Rue des Saint-Pères, 75007 Paris
01 45 48 54 67
debauve-et-gallais.fr/en

LA MAISON DU CHOCOLAT
Pile up on decadent boxes of ganaches and pralinés crafted by chef Nicolas Cloiseau, recipient of the Meilleur Ouvrier de France award.
225 Rue du Faubourg Saint-Honoré,
75008 Paris
01 42 27 39 44
lamaisonduchocolat.com

EDWART CHOCOLATIER-MARAIS
Local chocolate maker Edwart Yansané creates the most unique flavors from the finest single-origin chocolates around (plus he's very generous with his tastings—you must stop by!).
17 Rue Vielle du Temple, 75004 Paris
01 42 78 48 92
edwart.fr

DAMYEL
46 Rue des Rosiers, 75004 Paris
damyel.com

pastries, breads & sweets

AUX MERVEILLEUX DE FRED
One of my favorite things to pick up for an afternoon goûter is their raisin or chocolate cramique, usually served piping hot straight from the oven.
24 Rue du Pont Louis-Philippe,
75004 Paris
01 57 40 98 43
auxmerveilleux.com/home_en

BONESHAKER DOUGHNUTS
Classic donuts handcrafted by an American pastry chef.
77 Rue d'Aboukir, 75002 Paris
boneshakerparis.com

BONTEMPS PÂTISSERIE

Stop by for breathtaking sablés (some of the city's best!) and pastries served in a secret garden.

57 Rue de Bretagne, 75003 Paris
01 42 74 10 68
Instagram: bontempsparis

BOULANGERIE UTOPIE

Brave the lines for their signature black sesame–flavored pastries and unique specialty breads like baguette au charbon, using charcoal, and pain au thé vert sencha, a sencha green tea bread topped with toasted puffed rice.

20 Rue Jean-Pierre Timbaud,
75011 Paris
09 82 50 74 48

BOUTIQUE PIERRE HERMÉ

Home to the most exquisite confections in the city, crafted by the "Picasso of Pastry."

72 Rue Bonaparte, 75006 Paris
01 43 54 47 77
pierreherme.com

CEDRIC GROLET OPÉRA

Taste the celebrated pastry chef's magnificent modern interpretations of classic French desserts.

35 Avenue de l'Opéra, 75002 Paris
cedric-grolet.com

FOU DE PÂTISSERIE

A fabulous one-stop shop presenting a collection of creations from various pastry chefs, all in the same boutique.

45 Rue Montorgueil, 75002 Paris
foudepatisserieboutique.fr

DALLOYAU BOUTIQUE HISTORIQUE

Both my Gâteau Opéra (page 122) and Marble Tea Cake (page 53) found inspiration in the creations from this time-honored pâtisserie.

101 Rue du Faubourg Saint-Honoré,
75008 Paris
01 42 99 90 08
dalloyau.fr

DES GÂTEAUX ET DU PAIN

Seasonal fruits inspire the refined creations at this shop by award-winning pastry chef Claire Damon (so stop by every season to see what's new).

89 Rue du Bac, 75007 Paris
desgateauxetdupain.com

DU PAIN ET DES IDÉES

There's always a line out the door of this tiny boulangerie, and for good reason: Its chocolate-pistachio "escargot" pastry is astounding!

34 Rue Yves Toudic, 75010 Paris
01 42 40 44 52
dupainetdesidees.com

JACQUES GENIN

His caramel assortment is killer, but I go for the sparkling jewels he creates known as pâtes de fruits. Try the beetroot or rhubarb flavor.

133 Rue de Turenne, 75003 Paris
01 45 77 29 01
jacquesgenin.fr

MORI YOSHIDA

A spot near Les Invalides to check out, especially in summer when his fraisier— strawberry cake—is in season.

65 Avenue de Breteuil, 75007 Paris
01 47 34 29 74
moriyoshida.fr

POILÂNE

Three generations of Parisian bakers who have perfected the art of bread making. I never leave without picking up a flaky, buttery chausson aux pommes, or apple turnover!

38 Rue Debelleyme, 75003 Paris
01 44 61 83 39
poilane.com

POPELINI

Specializing in a crowd-pleasing variety of cream puffs, this shop found its name in Catherine de Médicis's Italian chef, who invented pate a choux in 1540.

35 Rue de Turenne, 75003 Paris
01 48 04 06 81
Instagram: popeliniofficiel

LA MAISON DU MOCHI

If you are a mochi aficionado like me, you'll delight in the offerings of this pretty boutique, home to the city's best mochi.

120 Rue de Turenne, 75003 Paris
09 80 48 42 53
maisondumochi.fr

STOHRER

Marvel at the oldest pâtisserie in Paris, serving up pastry perfection since 1730. Try the puits d'amour, a specialty of the shop and a personal favorite. The name translates to "well of love," a fitting name for this puff pastry confection filled with caramelized pastry cream.

51 Rue Montorgueil, 75002 Paris
01 42 33 38 20
stohrer.fr

tearooms & afternoon tea

ANGELINA PARIS

Order the legendary tearoom's famous hot chocolate "L'Africain," made with carefully selected cocoas from Niger, Ghana, and the Côte d'Ivoire, in a secret blend specially put together for Angelina, and their signature Mont-Blanc pastry.

226 Rue de Rivoli, 75001 Paris
01 42 60 82 00
angelina-paris.fr/en

MARIAGE FRÈRES

While there are numerous branches of this historic tea house scattered throughout Paris, my favorite location for afternoon tea is at Rue des Grands Augustins. Nab a table near the window and sip their signature Marco Polo tea in bliss.

13 Rue des Grands Augustins,
75006 Paris
01 40 51 82 50
mariagefreres.com

THE FOUR SEASONS GEORGE V

Take your afternoon tea in La Galerie, the all-day lounge in the heart of the famous palace hotel where you can indulge in head pastry chef Michael Bartocetti's beautiful creations.

31 Avenue George V, 75008 Paris
01 49 52 70 06
fourseasons.com/paris/dining

THE RITZ PARIS

Try Chef François Perret's award-winning pastries at either the Salon Proust or the Bar Vendôme.

15 Place Vendôme, 75001 Paris
01 43 16 33 74
ritzparis.com/en-GB/salon-proust

HÔTEL DE CRILLON

A formal tea at the Jardin d'Hiver inside this legendary five-star palace hotel includes a splendid selection of savories and sweets by head pastry chef Matthieu Carlin.

10 Place de la Concorde, 75008 Paris
01 44 71 15 00
rosewoodhotels.com/en/hotel
-de-crillon/dining/jardin-d-hiver

CHEVAL BLANC PARIS

At the time of this writing, Paris is eagerly anticipating the opening of this luxury hotel, where pastry chef Maxime Frédéric, formerly of the Four Seasons, will be spearheading the tastes of what promises to be a decadent teatime overlooking the Seine.

8 Quai du Louvre, 75001 Paris
01 40 28 00 00
chevalblanc.com

LE LOIR DANS LA THÉIÈRE

Stop by for a slice of the signature tarte au citron with mile-high meringue.

3 Rue des Rosiers, 75004 Paris
01 42 72 90 61
leloirdanslatheiere.com

shopping

ASTIER DE VILLATTE

This beautiful homeware boutique is where I bought some of the ceramic cake stands featured throughout the book.

173 Rue Saint-Honoré, 75001 Paris
01 42 60 74 13
astierdevillatte.com

TRUDON

This shop combines elegance and history to create candles I love to display at home (you'll spot them in the Fêtes chapter!).

11 Rue Sainte-Croix de la Bretonnerie, 75004 Paris
01 42 77 90 88
trudon.com

E.DEHILLERIN

Browse the copper-filled aisles of Paris's oldest cookware shop.

18-20 Rue Coquillière, 75001 Paris
01 42 36 53 13
edehillerin.fr/en

FROMAGERIE LAURENT DUBOIS

A refined shop of very special cheeses from a master fromager honored with the prestigious Meilleur Ouvrier de France award.

97-99 Rue Saint-Antoine, 75004
01 48 87 17 10
fromageslaurentdubois.fr

L'ARROSOIR

You'll always get gorgeous blooms at this dreamy hundred-year-old floral shop, now owned by American (and California girl!) Adrienne Ryser.

80 Rue Oberkampf, 75011 Paris
01 43 57 15 61
larrosoirparis.com

LA CHAMBRE AUX CONFITURES

There's an eye-popping amount of seasonal and unique French-made jams to be discovered at this sweet shop in the Marais.

60 Rue Vieille du Temple, 75003
01 79 25 53 58
lachambreauxconfitures.com/en

LA GRANDE ÉPICERIE

Find almost every French foodie brand you're dreaming of in this massive grocery store linked to the legendary Bon Marché department store in the 7th.

38 Rue de Sèvres, 75007 Paris
01 44 39 81 00
lagrandeepicerie.com

LIBRAIRIE GALIGNANI

There's nothing lovelier than lingering in the English section of this hidden gem of a bookstore.

224 Rue de Rivoli, 75001 Paris
01 42 60 76 07
galignani.fr

MADAME DE LA MAISON

Gorgeous French linens and antiques sourced by friend and style maven Ajiri Aki to help you create memorable moments.

madamedelamaison.com

MARIN MONTAGUT

This inspired housewares boutique owned by illustrator and designer Marin Montagut brings his brand of bohemian whimsy to the Left Bank.

48 Rue Madame, 75006 Paris
09 81 22 53 44
marinmontagut.com

OGATA

A chic emporium to all things Japan. I come here to buy specialty tea from Kyoto and shop for beautiful Japanese ceramics.

16 Rue Debelleyme, 75003 Paris
ogata.com

acknowledgments

MERCI BEAUCOUP TO . . .

My agent, Leigh Eisenman. Without you this book would never have been made. You believed in this project even before I did. Thank you for the numerous pep talks, brainstorming sessions, and buttercream appreciation texts! I'm grateful we've had cake dates in both Paris and New York, and I look forward to many more.

My mother for imparting her love of cake. Thank you for teaching me early on that it isn't a party unless there's dessert!

My Australian cake sister, Jennifer Drew. For always pushing me to be a better cake maker and providing endless encouragement whenever I doubted myself.

To all my friends in Paris who have helped make the city feel like home these last ten years and who are always willing to pop by to try my latest creation, but especially Amy Feezor for your wit and wisdom with words! Thank you for helping me tell my story so beautifully. It was a joy to stroll through all the seasons of Paris with you.

Beth Hewitt for your willingness to lend a hand (literally) in not one but two cake scenes, best madeleine model ever, and for your brilliant maneuvering through the boulevards of Paris as you kindly delivered us to various location shoots around the city!

Lindsey Tramuta for your sage advice on pretty much everything from taste-testing, head-note reviewing, and photography selection. You kept me laughing through some tough moments, you're a keeper!

My photographer and friend Joann Pai for agreeing to spend a year shooting bundts, butter-cream, and bûche all while simultaneously handling the arrival of your first child! I'm in awe of your talents.

Kate Devine for your meticulous styling eye and knowing everything from how to prop up a tilting cake stand to emergency repairs on broken pear stems!

Cristina Garces for your early enthusiasm for this book. Elinor Hutton for your expert editing; I know some of my recipes are lengthy! The entire team at Harper Design, especially Marta Schooler and Lynne Yeamans for helping me bring this book to life, and Soyolmaa Lkhagvadorj for always bringing such excitement to our calls and making the whole process so much fun.

Lauren Salkeld for saving me on countless occasions during recipe development. I wouldn't have found my way out of conversion chaos without you!

Un grand merci to Amanda Jane Jones for lending a fresh and fun vibe to the design of this book, bravo!

Rosie Kiser Jones for your charming illustrations that I am absolutely smitten with!

All the friends and family who assisted me during the recipe testing stage but especially Alexander Roberts, Jen Drew, Claudia and Sara Lieberman, Frederic, Zoé and Morganne Rose, Lorie Durnan, and Sarah Dapcevich.

And finally to my wonderful husband, James, for being the best CEO (Chief of Everything Officer). From reading early drafts to consuming countless cake tops and keeping Fitzgerald entertained on our endless shoot days. Thank you for your unending patience and support, je t'aime!

index

ABOUT THE AUTHOR Southern California native Frank Barron moved to Paris in 2012. He began baking in Paris simply to satisfy his craving for the desserts he'd grown up enjoying in the US and has become a sought-after baker and influencer, amassing a devoted following as @cakeboyparis on Instagram. He has been featured in publications including *Bake from Scratch*, *Time Out Paris*, and *Saveur*, and has partnered with brands including Le Bon Marché Rive Gauche and Kitchen Aid France. He lives in the Marais district with his husband, James, and his Boston terrier, Fitz, who are always willing to taste test his latest creations.